T0215420

Creating ASP.NET Core Web Applications

Proven Approaches to Application Design and Development

Dirk Strauss

Apress®

Creating ASP.NET Core Web Applications: Proven Approaches to Application Design and Development

Dirk Strauss
Uitenhage, South Africa

ISBN-13 (pbk): 978-1-4842-6827-8   ISBN-13 (electronic): 978-1-4842-6828-5
https://doi.org/10.1007/978-1-4842-6828-5

Managing Director, Apress Media LLC: Welmoed Spahr
Acquisitions Editor: Smriti Srivastava
Development Editor: Laura Berendson
Coordinating Editor: Shrikant Vishwakarma

Cover designed by eStudioCalamar

Cover image designed by Pexels

Distributed to the book trade worldwide by Springer Science+Business Media LLC, 1 New York Plaza, Suite 4600, New York, NY 10004. Phone 1-800-SPRINGER, fax (201) 348-4505, e-mail orders-ny@springer-sbm.com, or visit www.springeronline.com. Apress Media, LLC is a California LLC and the sole member (owner) is Springer Science + Business Media Finance Inc (SSBM Finance Inc). SSBM Finance Inc is a **Delaware** corporation.

For information on translations, please e-mail booktranslations@springernature.com; for reprint, paperback, or audio rights, please e-mail bookpermissions@springernature.com, or visit http://www.apress.com/rights-permissions.

Apress titles may be purchased in bulk for academic, corporate, or promotional use. eBook versions and licenses are also available for most titles. For more information, reference our Print and eBook Bulk Sales web page at http://www.apress.com/bulk-sales.

Any source code or other supplementary material referenced by the author in this book is available to readers on GitHub via the book's product page, located at www.apress.com/978-1-4842-6827-8. For more detailed information, please visit http://www.apress.com/source-code.

Printed on acid-free paper

For Adele, Irénéé, and Tristan. You are my everything.

Table of Contents

About the Author

Dirk Strauss is a software developer from South Africa who has been writing code since 2003. He has extensive experience in SYSPRO, with C# and web development being his main focus. He studied at the Nelson Mandela University, where he wrote software on a part-time basis to gain a better understanding of the technology. He remains passionate about writing code and imparting what he learns to others.

About the Technical Reviewer

 **Carsten Thomsen** is a back-end developer primarily but working with smaller front-end bits as well. He has authored and reviewed a number of books and created numerous Microsoft Learning courses, all to do with software development. He works as a freelancer/contractor in various countries in Europe; Azure, Visual Studio, Azure DevOps, and GitHub are some of the tools he works with. Being an exceptional troubleshooter, asking the right questions, including the less logical ones, in a most logical to least logical fashion, he also enjoys working with architecture, research, analysis, development, testing, and bug fixing. Carsten is a very good communicator with great mentoring and team-lead skills, and great skills in researching and presenting new material.

Acknowledgments

I would like to thank my wife and kids for their support during the writing of this book. I love you always!

Introduction

.NET Core has given .NET developers a lot to think about. Some developers have embraced the technology, while others have taken a wait-and-see approach. Whatever approach you are taking, .NET Core is without a doubt here to stay.

Developing web applications is also not one of the easiest things to do. I've always wanted to write a book on developing web applications, but to do it in a way that is very structured and takes the reader on a journey of discovery.

Creating ASP.NET Core Web Applications is my attempt at that book. I always try to take the point of view that the book I'm writing is a reference book for my bookshelf. With this in mind, I, therefore, tried to cover a wide set of topics.

As with all projects, Chapter 1 starts with creating your project and using the .NET CLI. We have a look at adding Razor pages and also how to configure the application using the appsettings.json file. I then create a dummy data service, which is used to get the application up and running with test data. This test data is designed in such a way that it can easily be swapped out at a later stage (and I show you how to do this).

Chapter 2 takes a look at the process of creating models, model binding, tag helpers, working with a query string, and page routes. To illustrate these concepts, Chapter 2 shows you how to implement a search form. This allows us to search for data, view the details, and add in logic to handle bad requests.

Chapter 3 illustrates the concepts of editing the data, displaying validation errors, and modifying the data access service to suit our needs. I also discuss the differences between singleton, scoped, and transient lifetime registration for services.

EF Core and SQL Server become the focus in the next chapter. Chapter 4 shows you how to install Entity Framework Core, define your connection strings, what database migrations are, and how to use them. We will also be implementing a new data access service and changing the data access service registration from the test data to the SQL data.

Moving to the front end next, we have a look at working with Razor pages in Chapter 5. Here, we will look at what sections are and how they benefit you as a developer. We take a closer look at _ViewImports and _ViewStart files. I also show you how to create your own tag helper, how to work with partial views, and, finally, how to work with ViewComponents.

Staying front end, we have a look at adding client-side logic in Chapter 6. I show you how to separate production scripts from development scripts, use SCSS to generate CSS, how SCSS works, and the different features you can use to create CSS with SCSS, as well as work with Chrome Developer Tools. This is, in my opinion, crucial for any web developer to know.

With Chapter 7, we will take a look at what middleware is. This is a very important chapter and one that will require some explaining. We have a look at some of the built-in middleware components, but also how to create a custom middleware component if the built-in middleware components don't suit your needs. After creating a custom middleware component, we will have a look at logging in ASP.NET Core. Logging is a big subject, but this book tries to cover the basics.

Finally, Chapter 8 will take you through getting your web application ready for deployment and finally publishing your web application and hooking it up to a SQL Server database. I hope that you will enjoy this book as much as I enjoyed writing it.

CHAPTER 1

Creating and Setting Up Your Project

Welcome to Creating ASP.NET Core Web Applications! This book will guide you through creating a typical ASP.NET Core Web Application, from start to finish. All the code illustrated in this book is available on GitHub and will be an invaluable resource to you as you navigate the code samples in the book.

This chapter will take you through the steps required to start your web application development. We will also have a look at adding and editing Razor pages, working with Entities, creating and registering a data service, and using that data service to display test data on the web page.

Creating Your Web Application Project

In this book, I will be using Visual Studio 2019 to illustrate the concepts surrounding ASP.NET Core Web Applications. For those folks that do not use Visual Studio, the same result as detailed in the following can be achieved for creating an application by using the .NET CLI.

I will assume that you have already installed .NET Core onto your machine. The web application we will be creating will use .NET Core 3.1. If you have not installed .NET Core, you can do so by visiting this link: `https://dotnet.microsoft.com/download`.

Because we are working with .NET Core which is cross-platform, I will also show you how to create an application using the Command Prompt later in this section.

1

© Dirk Strauss 2021
D. Strauss, *Creating ASP.NET Core Web Applications*, https://doi.org/10.1007/978-1-4842-6828-5_1

For now, let us start by creating a new project in Visual Studio. From the file menu, click New Project. This will display the Create a new project screen as seen in Figure 1-1.

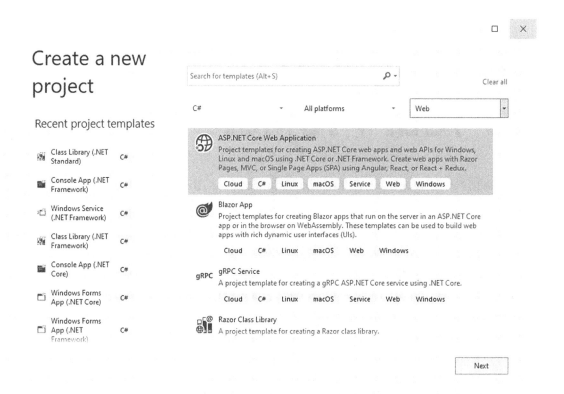

Figure 1-1. *The Create New Project Screen*

The Create a new project screen that allows you to select the correct project template lists all the available templates included in Visual Studio. In our case, we will be using the ASP.NET Core Web Application template.

If you are used to working in previous versions of Visual Studio, you will notice that this screen has been vastly improved. You can search for templates by typing a template name into the search text box or by holding down Alt+S.

You can also filter project templates from the drop-downs on the form. You will notice that you can filter by language, platform, and project type.

Clicking the Next button will take you to the Configure your new project screen as seen in Figure 1-2.

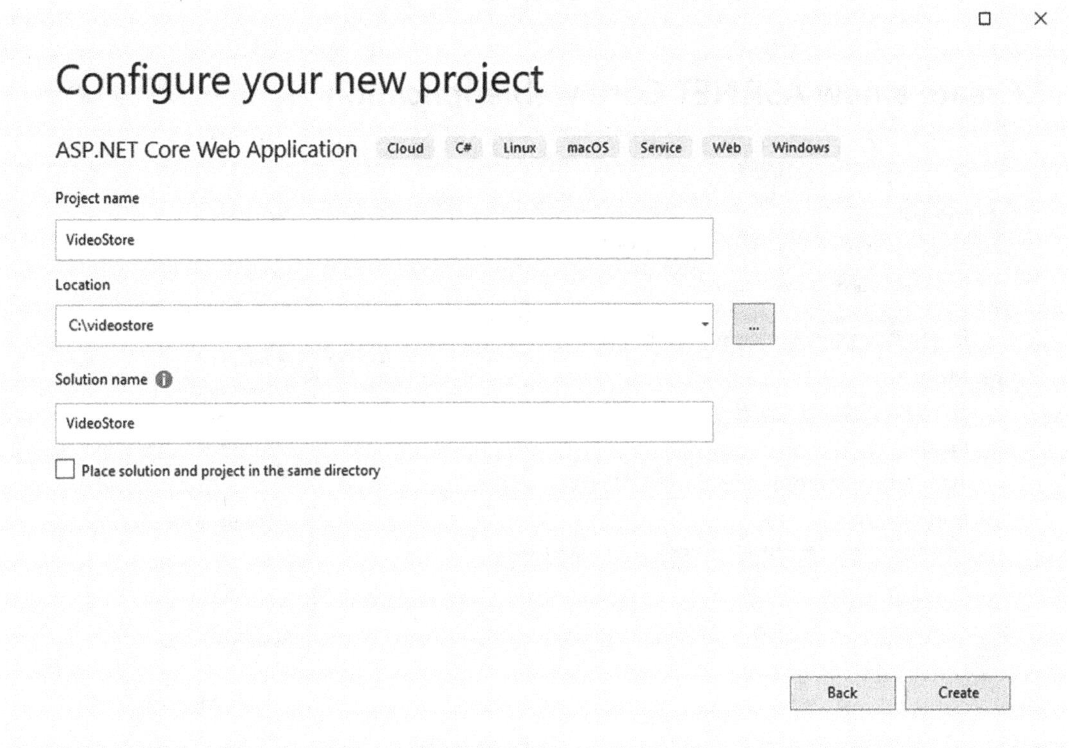

□   ✕

Configure your new project

ASP.NET Core Web Application   Cloud   C#   Linux   macOS   Service   Web   Windows

Project name

VideoStore

Location

C:\videostore

Solution name ⓘ

VideoStore

☐ Place solution and project in the same directory

Back   Create

Figure 1-2. *Configure Your New Project*

Give the project a suitable name. For this book, we will simply call the project VideoStore and specify a location to create the project in. When you have done this, click the Create button.

You will now be taken to a second screen as seen in Figure 1-3 where you can select the specific type of template that you want to use.

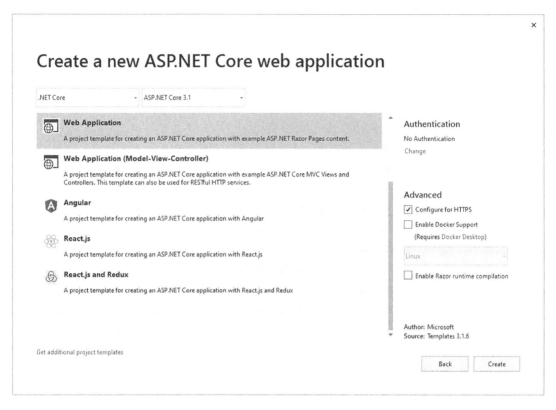

Figure 1-3. *Selecting a Specific Template Type*

It is here that we can specify the version of .NET Core that we want to use. In this example, we are selecting .NET Core 3.1. We can then tell Visual Studio that we want to create a basic web application. Just leave the rest of the settings at their default values and click the Create button.

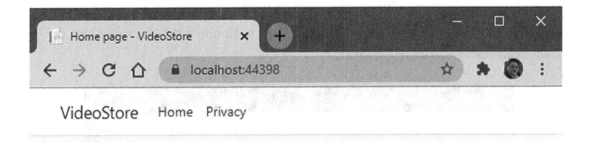

Figure 1-4. *Running the Web Application*

After the project has been created in Visual Studio, you can hit Ctrl+F5 to run the web application. This will run your project without the debugger attached and display the web application in your browser as seen in Figure 1-4.

You will notice that the web application is running on port 44398 in this example, but your port will most likely be different. By default, this web application includes some basic features such as a Home page as well as a Privacy page.

It is from here that we will start to flesh out our web application and add more features and functionality to it.

Using the .NET CLI

Earlier in this chapter, I mentioned that we can also create the project from the Command Prompt. Therefore, for those of you that do not use Visual Studio, the .NET CLI offers a cross-platform way for creating .NET Core projects.

Once you have installed .NET Core on your Mac, Linux, or Windows machine, you should be able to simply open your Terminal, Shell, or Command Prompt and type the dotnet command as seen in Figure 1-5.

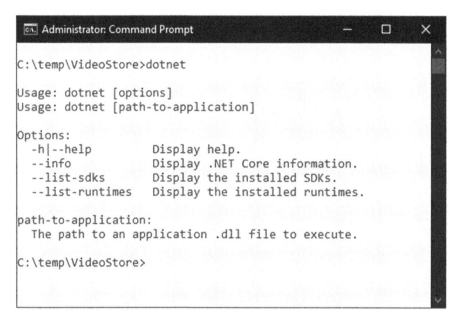

Figure 1-5. *Running the dotnet Command*

To see more of the commands available with dotnet, you can type dotnet -h in the Command Prompt. If you typed in dotnet new, you would see all the available project templates listed in your Command Prompt window.

These templates, along with the short name associated with that specific template, are listed in the following table.

Templates	Short Name	Language	Tags
Console Application	Console	C#, F#, VB	Common/ Console
Class library	classlib	C#, F#, VB	Common/ Library
WPF Application	wpf	C#	Common/WPF
WPF Class library	wpflib	C#	Common/WPF

(*continued*)

Templates	Short Name	Language	Tags
WPF Custom Control Library	wpfcustomcontrollib	C#	Common/WPF
WPF User Control Library	wpfusercontrollib	C#	Common/WPF
Windows Forms (WinForms) Application	winforms	C#	Common/WinForms
Windows Forms (WinForms) Class library	winformslib	C#	Common/WinForms
Worker Service	worker	C#	Common/Worker/Web
Unit Test Project	mstest	C#, F#, VB	Test/MSTest
NUnit 3 Test Project	nunit	C#, F#, VB	Test/NUnit
NUnit 3 Test Item	nunit-test	C#, F#, VB	Test/NUnit
xUnit Test Project	xunit	C#, F#, VB	Test/xUnit
Razor Component	razorcomponent	C#	Web/ASP.NET
Razor Page	page	C#	Web/ASP.NET
MVC ViewImports	viewimports	C#	Web/ASP.NET
MVC ViewStart	viewstart	C#	Web/ASP.NET
Blazor Server App	blazorserver	C#	Web/Blazor
Blazor WebAssembly App	blazorwasm	C#	Web/Blazor/WebAssembly
ASP.NET Core Empty	web	C#, F#	Web/Empty
ASP.NET Core Web App (Model-View-Controller)	mvc	C#, F#	Web/MVC
ASP.NET Core Web App	webapp	C#	Web/MVC/Razor Pages
ASP.NET Core with Angular	angular	C#	Web/MVC/SPA
ASP.NET Core with React.js	React	C#	Web/MVC/SPA
ASP.NET Core with React.js and Redux	Reactredux	C#	Web/MVC/SPA

(continued)

Templates	Short Name	Language	Tags
Razor Class Library	Razorclasslib	C#	Web/Razor/ Library/ Razor Class Library
ASP.NET Core Web API	Webapi	C#, F#	Web/WebAPI
ASP.NET Core gRPC Service	Grpc	C#	Web/gRPC
dotnet gitignore file	gitignore		Config
global.json file	globaljson		Config
NuGet Config	nugetconfig		Config
Dotnet local tool manifest file	tool-manifest		Config
Web Config	webconfig		Config
Solution File	sln		Solution

You will notice that to create an ASP.NET Web Application, we need to specify the short name webapp with the new command.

As seen in Figure 1-6, typing in the command dotnet new webapp will create the ASP.NET Web Application inside the current directory.

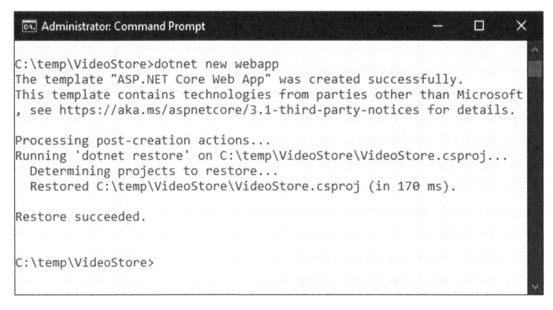

Figure 1-6. *Creating the Web App via the .NET CLI*

If you had to compare the project created via the .NET CLI with the one created in Visual Studio, you will see that these are identical.

The .NET CLI offers a fantastic, quick, and cross-platform way of creating applications.

Adding and Editing Razor Pages

With your web application running, you will notice that if you click the Privacy link in the navigation menu, it will go to the following URL: `https://localhost:44398/Privacy`. The web application is mapping the request created by clicking the Privacy link with the Razor pages in your VideoStore project. Looking at Figure 1-7, you will see the Razor pages in a folder called... you guessed it, Pages.

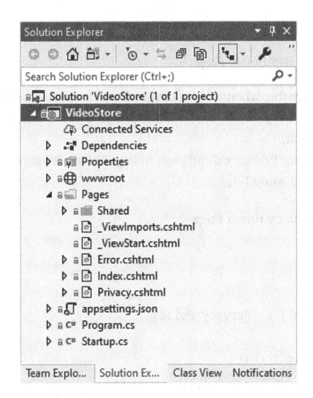

Figure 1-7. *The Razor Pages in the Solution Explorer*

This means that when I view the Privacy page in the web application, ASP.NET Core is busy rendering the Privacy.cshtml page. You will also notice that the cshtml extension is not required in the URL as seen in Figure 1-8.

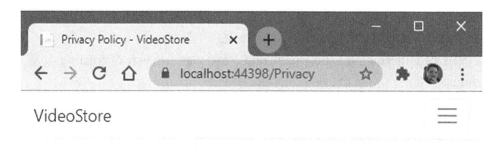

Figure 1-8. *The Privacy Policy Page*

You will also notice that when you make your browser window smaller, the menu collapses into the hamburger icon. This is made possible by Bootstrap, which is included in the project by default.

If you now click your Privacy.cshtml page in the Solution Explorer, you will see the code as listed in Code Listing 1-1.

Listing 1-1. The Privacy Razor Page

```
@page
@model PrivacyModel
@{
    ViewData["Title"] = "Privacy Policy";
}
<h1>@ViewData["Title"]</h1>

<p>Use this page to detail your site's privacy policy.</p>
```

With your web application running without the debugger attached, if you click the hamburger menu icon, you will see that we have just two pages listed which are Home and Privacy.

Looking at Figure 1-9 and comparing that to the code in Code Listing 1-1, you might be wondering where the code is for the navigation.

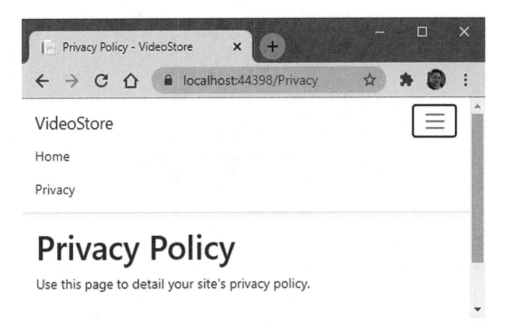

Figure 1-9. *The Navigation Menu*

The answer lies in a special Razor page called a Layout page. Swing back to your Solution Explorer, and expand the Shared folder under the Pages folder. There you will see a page called _Layout.cshtml as seen in Figure 1-10.

Figure 1-10. *The Shared Layout Page*

It is this Layout page that renders everything within the web application's <head> tags, things such as links to all the required stylesheets, as well as <body> tags that include a <header> section containing the navigation menu. The code for the navigation menu is listed in Code Listing 1-2.

Listing 1-2. The Navigation Menu Code

```
<div class="navbar-collapse collapse d-sm-inline-flex flex-sm-row-reverse">
  <ul class="navbar-nav flex-grow-1">
    <li class="nav-item"><a class="nav-link text-dark" asp-area="" asp-
    page="/Index">Home</a></li>
    <li class="nav-item"><a class="nav-link text-dark" asp-area="" asp-
    page="/Privacy">Privacy</a></li>
  </ul>
</div>
```

Go ahead and add another menu item called Videos, by adding a new list item to the unordered list as seen in Code Listing 1-3.

Listing 1-3. Modified Navigation Menu Code

```
<div class="navbar-collapse collapse d-sm-inline-flex flex-sm-row-reverse">
  <ul class="navbar-nav flex-grow-1">
    <li class="nav-item"><a class="nav-link text-dark" asp-area="" asp-
    page="/Index">Home</a></li>
    <li class="nav-item"><a class="nav-link text-dark" asp-area="" asp-
    page="/ Videos/List">Videos</a></li>
    <li class="nav-item"><a class="nav-link text-dark" asp-area="" asp-
    page="/Privacy">Privacy</a></li>
  </ul>
</div>
```

You will notice that the `asp-page` tag helper specifies `Videos/List` which tells my web application that inside a folder called Videos is a page that will display a list of videos. Running your web application again, you will see that the Videos menu item has been added to the navigation menu (Figure 1-11).

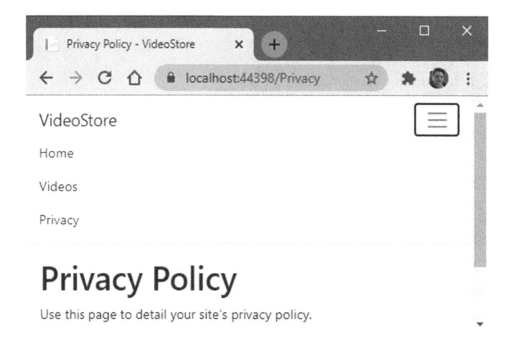

Figure 1-11. *Navigation Menu Modified*

If you click the Videos menu item, the link will not navigate anywhere. This is because we have not yet added the required Razor page. As shown in Figure 1-12, add a new folder under the Pages folder in your Solution Explorer.

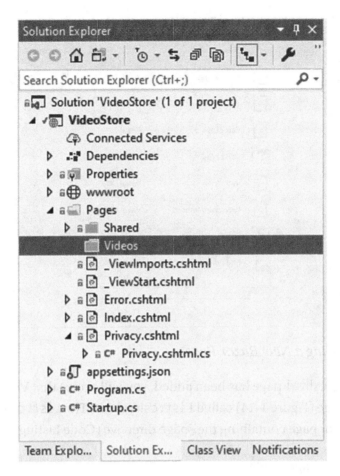

Figure 1-12. *Adding the Videos Folder*

Next, right-click the Videos folder, and add a new Razor page called List to the folder. This can be done from the context menu or from the Add New Item screen as shown in Figure 1-13.

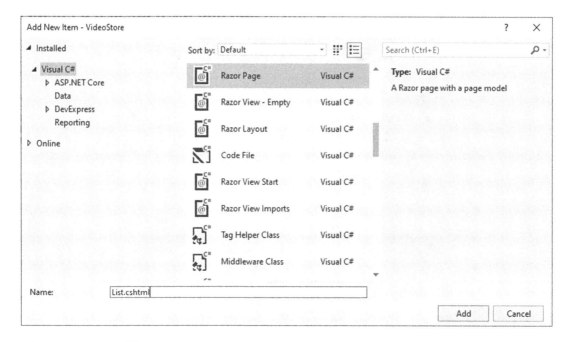

Figure 1-13. *Adding a New Razor Page*

Once the `List.cshtml` page has been added, you will notice that Visual Studio has added a second page (Figure 1-14) called `List.cshtml.cs`. The `List.cshtml` file is essentially my Razor page containing the `@page` directive (Code Listing 1-4).

Listing 1-4. Razor Page Code

```
@page
@model VideoStore.Pages.Videos.ListModel
@{
}
```

Furthermore, the Razor page also specifies a model with the `@model` directive. It is telling .NET Core that the model that contains video information is contained in an object of type `ListModel`.

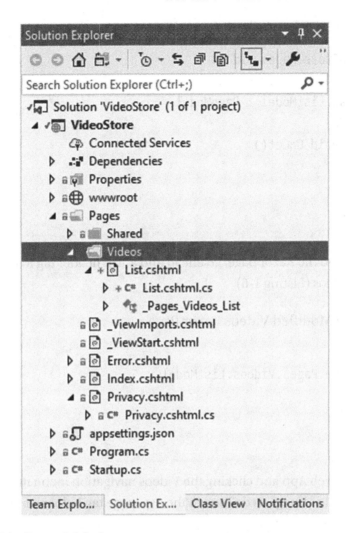

Figure 1-14. *List Page Added*

This ListModel is the class contained in the List.cshtml.cs file nested under the List.cshtml page. Looking at the code listing in Listing 1-5, it is interesting to notice that the ListModel class inherits from an abstract class called PageModel.

Listing 1-5. The ListModel Class

```
namespace VideoStore.Pages.Videos
{
    public class ListModel : PageModel
    {
        public void OnGet()
        {
        }
    }
}
```

Swinging back to the Razor page, go ahead and add a header tag to give the page a heading called Videos (Listing 1-6).

Listing 1-6. The Modified Videos Razor Page

```
@page
@model VideoStore.Pages.Videos.ListModel
@{
}

<h1>Videos</h1>
```

Running your Web App and clicking the Videos navigation menu item, you will be taken to the Video List page as defined in the asp-page tag helper earlier.

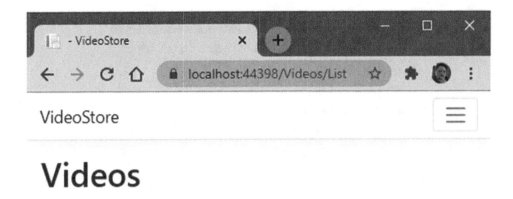

Figure 1-15. *Videos List Page*

Referring to Figure 1-15, you will notice that the browser is displaying the Videos/List URL.

Looking at the Configuration

Inside your VideoStore project, you will notice a file (Figure 1-16) called `appsettings.json`. This is your application's configuration file and can easily be referenced from within your Razor page.

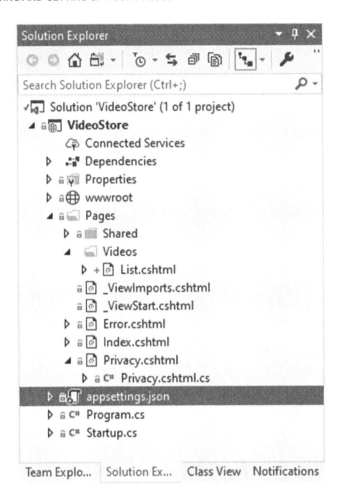

Figure 1-16. *The appsettings.json Configuration File*

The appsettings.json is one of the sources of configuration in your application. This means that anything I add to this file can be used when your web application runs.

Listing 1-7. The appsettings.json File

```
{
  "Logging": {
    "LogLevel": {
      "Default": "Information",
      "Microsoft": "Warning",
      "Microsoft.Hosting.Lifetime": "Information"
    }
```

```
  },
  "AllowedHosts": "*"
}
```

Opening up the file (Code Listing 1-7), you will see that it contains JSON, and I can easily add additional settings here.

Listing 1-8. Modified appsettings.json File

```
{
  "Logging": {
    "LogLevel": {
      "Default": "Information",
      "Microsoft": "Warning",
      "Microsoft.Hosting.Lifetime": "Information"
    }
  },
  "AllowedHosts": "*",
  "VideoListPageTitle":  "Video Store - Videos List"
}
```

Modify the `appsettings.json` file by adding a `VideoListPageTitle` property with a value of `Video Store - Videos List` as seen in Listing 1-8. To display the `VideoListPageTitle` property on my Razor page, I need to modify my `ListModel` class.

Razor pages are only concerned with displaying data. It is the responsibility of the ListModel class to fetch the data required to display on the Razor page.

If you look back at Code Listing 1-5, you will notice that the `ListModel` class specifies a `public void OnGet()` method. It is this method that will respond to `HTTP GET` requests, and it is here that we will modify the code slightly to get the data for the page title from our configuration file.

To get the setting in the configuration file, we need to expose this configuration file to our `ListModel` class by passing a parameter of type `IConfiguration` into the `ListModel` constructor. Go ahead and modify your ListModel class as seen in Code Listing 1-9.

Listing 1-9. The Modified ListModel Class

```
public class ListModel : PageModel
{
    private readonly IConfiguration _config;

    public string PageTitle { get; set; }

    public ListModel(IConfiguration config)
    {
        _config = config;
    }

    public void OnGet()
    {
        PageTitle = _config["VideoListPageTitle"];
    }
}
```

You will notice that I have added a constructor that takes a parameter of type
IConfiguration, a private field called _config, as well as a property called PageTitle.

You might need to bring in the Microsoft.Extensions.Configuration namespace in
your using statements to reference IConfiguration.

Then, in the OnGet method, I can get the value stored in the configuration file simply
by referencing the property, VideoListPageTitle added to the configuration file earlier
in Code Listing 1-8.

Because my ListModel class exposes the PageTitle property, which is being set in
the OnGet method, I can easily grab this value on my Razor page by using @Model (notice
the upper case M).

Listing 1-10. Displaying the PageTitle on the Razor Page

```
@page
@model VideoStore.Pages.Videos.ListModel
@{
}

<h1>@Model.PageTitle</h1>
```

As seen in Code Listing 1-10, when I dot after typing @Model, I will see the PageTitle property displayed in Visual Studio's IntelliSense.

Figure 1-17. *The Videos List Page Title Displayed*

Running the web application and navigating to the Videos page, you will see the page title displayed that we set in the configuration file (Figure 1-17).

Working with Entities

To explain the concept of Entities, we need to understand what an Entity is. Our Videos/ List page has now been created and will be used to display a list of videos, but we need a way to define exactly what a Video is. This is essentially what the job of the Entity is.

To separate the different application concerns in our web application, go ahead and add a new project to the solution by right-clicking the solution and selecting Add, New Project from the context menu.

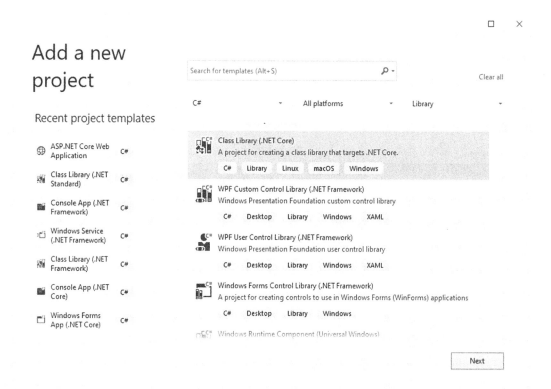

Figure 1-18. *Add a New Project*

You will then see the Add a new project window pop up (Figure 1-18). From the list of project templates, select a .NET Core Class Library, and click the Next button.

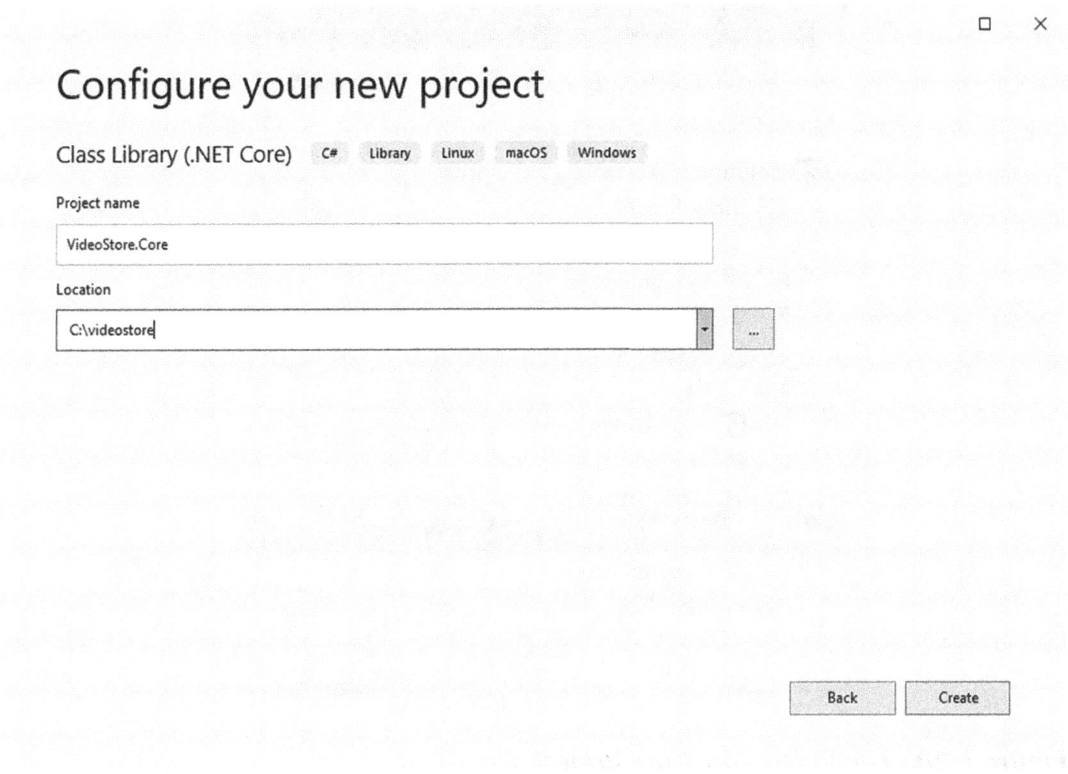

□   ✕

Configure your new project

Class Library (.NET Core)   C#   Library   Linux   macOS   Windows

Project name

VideoStore.Core

Location

C:\videostore   ▾   ...

Back   Create

Figure 1-19. *Adding a .NET Core Class Library*

Call the project VideoStore.Core, and click the Create button (Figure 1-19). It is this project that will contain the classes that represent the core of our VideoStore application. Therefore, this project will contain such things as the Entities we will need to use.

Figure 1-20. *The VideoStore.Core Project*

After adding this project, you will notice in Figure 1-20 that the class name defaults to Class1.cs. Because our project is concerned with Videos, we will rename this class to Video.cs (singular) as seen in Listing 1-11.

Listing 1-11. The Video Class

```
namespace VideoStore.Core
{
    public class Video
    {
    }
}
```

We now have an entity that will define exactly what a Video looks like. Let's add some properties to the Video class to define what it looks like. These can be seen in Code Listing 1-12.

You can add as many properties as you like, but to keep things simple, I will just add a basic set of properties to define our Video class.

Listing 1-12. The Video Class Properties

```
namespace VideoStore.Core
{
    public class Video
    {
        public int Id { get; set; }
        public string Title { get; set; }
        public DateTime ReleaseDate { get; set; }
    }
}
```

There is one more file that I will want to add to define the different movie genres. This file will be called MovieGenre.cs and will contain an enum as illustrated in Code Listing 1-13.

Listing 1-13. The MovieGenre enum

```
namespace VideoStore.Core
{
    public enum MovieGenre
    {
        None,
        Action,
        Romance,
        Drama,
        Horror
    }
}
```

Your solution should now look as illustrated in Figure 1-21.

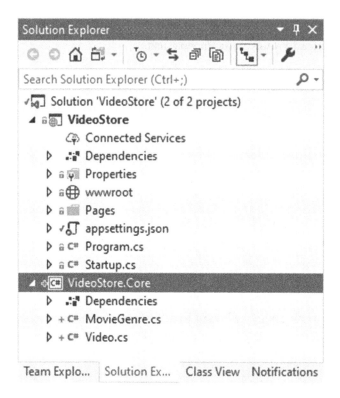

Figure 1-21. *The VideoStore.Core Project*

We now want to reference the MovieGenre enum in the Video class. Do this by adding a property of type MovieGenre as illustrated in Code Listing 1-14.

Listing 1-14. The Video Entity with a Property of Type MovieGenre

```csharp
namespace VideoStore.Core
{
    public class Video
    {
        public int Id { get; set; }
        public string Title { get; set; }
        public DateTime ReleaseDate { get; set; }
        public MovieGenre Genre { get; set; }
    }
}
```

This Video class or Entity now represents the Video data that we will be using inside our web application. It completely defines what a Video should look like.

Creating and Registering a Data Service

We now want to set up the code required to display the data of our videos on the web page. To do this, we will be creating a data service, but at this point, I don't want to go through all the steps to add SQL to the project (not yet anyway).

For now, we will just be adding code to display test data, and, by doing so, allow us to get all the other bits of code created for our web application. This test data will be created in such a way that it will allow us to easily swap out the test data for real data later on when all the sections of the web application have been completed.

It is here that you will see how Interfaces allow us to accomplish this. As before, to separate concerns inside our application, we will add another .NET Core Class Library project to our solution called VideoStore.Data and rename the default Class1.cs file to TestData.cs as seen in Figure 1-22.

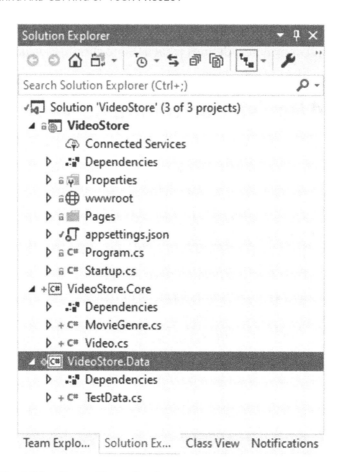

Figure 1-22. *The VideoStore.Data Project*

Next, add an Interface to your VideoStore.Data project by right-clicking your project and selecting Add, New Item from the context menu.

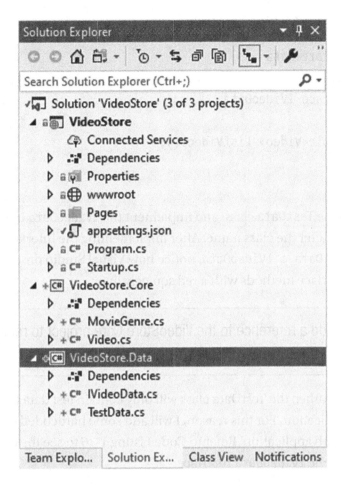

Figure 1-23. *The VideoStore.Data Project with the IVideoData Interface*

Our IVideoData Interface will tell our web application what methods need to be implemented in our data service (Figure 1-23). It is up to the TestData class to provide the implementation of the Interface, and this allows us to separate the TestData with actual data later on.

Open the IVideoData Interface, and add a method (Listing 1-15) that will return a list of videos to our page. It is important to note that the Interface does not tell us how to do something, but merely what to do. It will be up to the class (in this case the TestData class) that implements the Interface to determine exactly how the data is returned.

Listing 1-15. The IVideoData Interface

```
namespace VideoStore.Data
{
    public interface IVideoData
    {
        IEnumerable<Video> ListVideos();
    }
}
```

Swing over to the TestData class, and implement the IVideoData Interface by adding the Interface name after the class name. After implementing the Interface as follows, public class TestData : IVideoData, notice how Visual Studio prompts you to implement the Interface methods with a red squiggly line.

You will have to add a reference to the VideoStore.Core project to reference the Video entity.

As mentioned earlier, the TestData class will only contain test data to allow us to create our web application. For this reason, I will add some hardcoded data to simulate the videos in our web application. Refer to Code Listing 1-16 to see the complete implementation of the IVideoData Interface.

Listing 1-16. The TestData Class that Implements IVideoData

```
namespace VideoStore.Data
{
    public class TestData : IVideoData
    {
        List<Video> _videoList;
        public TestData()
        {
            _videoList = new List<Video>()
```

```
    {
        new Video { Id = 1, Title = "Movie Title 1", ReleaseDate =
        new DateTime(2018, 1, 21), Genre = MovieGenre.Action },
        new Video { Id = 2, Title = "Movie Title 2", ReleaseDate =
        new DateTime(2019, 7, 2), Genre = MovieGenre.Drama },
        new Video { Id = 3, Title = "Movie Title 3", ReleaseDate =
        new DateTime(2020, 2, 14), Genre = MovieGenre.Romance }
    };
    }
    public IEnumerable<Video> ListVideos() => _videoList.OrderBy(x =>
    x.Title);
    }
}
```

The next order of business is to display this data inside of our Razor page. It is now that I will be referencing the Interface instead of referencing the data directly. Referencing the Interface will allow me to swap out the data source later on when I am ready to work with a SQL Server database.

To get started with this, we need to open the Startup.cs file in the VideoStore project and look for a method called ConfigureServices (Listing 1-17). ASP.Net Core uses this method to determine all the services that your web application will need. It is here that I can notify my web application about my IVideoData Interface and tell it that whenever I want an object of IVideoData, it should provide me with my TestData.

Listing 1-17. The ConfigureServices Method

```
public void ConfigureServices(IServiceCollection services)
{
    _ = services.AddRazorPages();
}
```

To do this, I need to modify the ConfigureServices method and tell the services collection that whenever a page or component in my web application needs IVideoData, give it the TestData class.

You will need to add a reference to the VideoStore.Data project. Also note the use of the discard in Listing 1-17. The underscore is used to denote a discard when your method returns a value, but you do not intend using that value. In Listing 1-17, AddRazorPages returns an IMvcBuilder, but I am not using that to further configure the MVC services.

To do this, I add a scoped instance of my TestData service by modifying the code as illustrated in Code Listing 1-18. As a side note, the ConfigureServices method is used to register the services required by the app. ASP.NET Core then uses the built-in dependency injection framework to make these services available throughout your web application. To read up more about dependency injection in ASP.NET Core, have a look at the following link: https://docs.microsoft.com/en-us/aspnet/core/fundamentals/dependency-injection.

Listing 1-18. Modified ConfigureServices Method

```
public void ConfigureServices(IServiceCollection services)
{
    _ = services.AddScoped<IVideoData, TestData>();
    _ = services.AddRazorPages();
}
```

Now that I have my service registered, I can inject that into my ListModel class by modifying the constructor. Let's see how to do that next.

Displaying Test Data on Your Web Page

To consume the data service in my ListModel class, I can use dependency injection to inject my service in the constructor. You will recall that we previously injected the IConfiguration service when we were pulling values from the appsettings.json file.

Start by adding a reference to the VideoStore.Data project in the List.cshtml.cs file. Next, inject the IVideoData service in the constructor, and pass that off to a private field called _videoData. Your code should look as illustrated in Code Listing 1-19.

Listing 1-19. Modified ListModel Class

```
namespace VideoStore.Pages.Videos
{
    public class ListModel : PageModel
    {
        private readonly IConfiguration _config;
        private readonly IVideoData _videoData;

        public string PageTitle { get; set; }

        public ListModel(IConfiguration config, IVideoData videoData)
        {
            _config = config;
            _videoData = videoData;
        }
        public void OnGet()
        {
            PageTitle = _config["VideoListPageTitle"];
        }
    }
}
```

The ListModel class can now use the services we have injected to build up the data required to display on the Razor page. My Razor page can then use the public properties on the ListModel to pull that data and render it on the web page (the same way we exposed the PageTitle from the appsettings.json file).

The last two steps we need to complete on the ListModel are to add a public property to expose the video data to the Razor page and code to set that property in the OnGet method.

Go ahead and modify your ListModel class as illustrated in Code Listing 1-20. I have purposefully added the complete code file here so that you can see the using statements to the VideoStore.Core and VideoStore.Data projects.

Listing 1-20. Exposing the Video Data via a Property

```
using Microsoft.AspNetCore.Mvc.RazorPages;
using Microsoft.Extensions.Configuration;
using System.Collections.Generic;
using VideoStore.Core;
using VideoStore.Data;

namespace VideoStore.Pages.Videos
{
    public class ListModel : PageModel
    {
        private readonly IConfiguration _config;
        private readonly IVideoData _videoData;

        public string PageTitle { get; set; }
        public IEnumerable<Video> Videos { get; set; }

        public ListModel(IConfiguration config, IVideoData videoData)
        {
            _config = config;
            _videoData = videoData;
        }
        public void OnGet()
        {
            PageTitle = _config["VideoListPageTitle"];
            Videos = _videoData.ListVideos();
        }
    }
}
```

All that is left for us to do is to modify our Razor page to display the list of Videos on the web page. The great thing about Razor pages is that I can mix markup with C# and use it to loop collections, for example. All that I need to do is use the @ sign to switch between regular HTML markup and C#.

The code illustrated in Code Listing 1-21 uses a C# `foreach` statement to loop through the collection of videos in my test data source and output that on the Razor page.

Listing 1-21. The Razor Page Markup and C#

```
@page
@model VideoStore.Pages.Videos.ListModel
@{
}

<h1>@Model.PageTitle</h1>

<div class="container-fluid">
    <div class="row">
        <div class="col-md-4">
            Title
        </div>
        <div class="col-md-4">
            Release Date
        </div>
        <div class="col-md-4">
            Genre
        </div>
    </div>
    @foreach (var video in Model.Videos)
    {
        <div class="row">
            <div class="col-md-4">
                @video.Title
            </div>
            <div class="col-md-4">
                @video.ReleaseDate.ToShortDateString()
            </div>
            <div class="col-md-4">
                @video.Genre
            </div>
        </div>
    }
</div>
```

When I save all my work and run the web application, I will now see all the test data displayed on my web page (Figure 1-24).

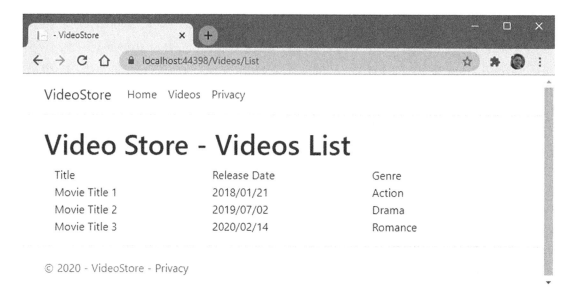

Figure 1-24. *The Test Data Displayed on the Videos List Page*

For now, this is perfect. I can continue to use this test data while I continue to develop my web application. When everything is completed, I can just swap out the data service via the IVideoData abstraction and switch from my test data to actual SQL data.

CHAPTER 2

Creating Models

In the previous chapter, we created logic to pull test data to our Video List form. That test data contained only three entries. Being test data, there is little need to add in a large volume of test data, not unless you want to test the responsiveness or speed of your page.

One thing that is therefore quite important is to add searching capabilities to our Video List form. This will allow the user to filter the list by some or other specific search queries.

Building a Search Form

I will be using Font Awesome icons in this application, so make sure that you have these set up. If you haven't set up Font Awesome, or want to use a different icon set, feel free to do so (this means you can skip the next section). For those that want to make use of Font Awesome, or haven't included an icon set in your application, let's see how to do that next.

Adding Font Awesome

The quickest way to add Font Awesome icons to your application is to use the CDN embed code. Point your browser to `https://fontawesome.com/start` and generate a Font Awesome Kit using your email address.

When you receive the confirmation email, verify your account, and then you will be taken to your kit code. The kit code will look similar to the code in Code Listing 2-1.

Listing 2-1. The Font Awesome Kit Code

```
<script src="https://kit.fontawesome.com/fec344983.js"
crossorigin="anonymous"></script>
```

Copy this script tag, and add it to the end of your scripts section, just above the `@RenderSection` in the `_Layout.cshtml` file.

© Dirk Strauss 2021
D. Strauss, *Creating ASP.NET Core Web Applications*, https://doi.org/10.1007/978-1-4842-6828-5_2

After adding this to the scripts section, your _Layout.cshtml page should look as in Code Listing 2-2.

Listing 2-2. Adding the Kit Code to Your Scripts Section

```
<footer class="border-top footer text-muted">
  <div class="container">
    &copy; 2020 - VideoStore - <a asp-area="" asp-page="/Privacy">Privacy</a>
  </div>
</footer>

<script src="~/lib/jquery/dist/jquery.min.js"></script>
<script src="~/lib/bootstrap/dist/js/bootstrap.bundle.min.js"></script>
<script src="~/js/site.js" asp-append-version="true"></script>

<script src="https://kit.fontawesome.com/fec344983.js"
crossorigin="anonymous"></script>

@RenderSection("Scripts", required: false)
```

This is all you need to do to make use of Font Awesome icons in your web application.

Adding the Search Form Code

Open the List.cshtml page, and have a look at the HTML markup contained therein. You will remember from Chapter 1 that it is here that we added the C# code mixed in with the markup to produce a grid layout of the videos contained in our test data.

Because this page lists all the videos in our Video Store, it makes sense to add the search functionality to this page. The code that we will be adding looks as illustrated in Code Listing 2-3.

Listing 2-3. The Search Form Code

```
<form method="get">
    <div class="form-group">
        <div class="input-group">
            <input type="search" class="form-control" value="" />
            <button class="btn btn-group">
```

```
            <i class="fas fa-search"></i>
        </button>
    </div>
</div>
</form>
```

Let's have a closer look at this code and expand a bit on what exactly we are doing here. In its most basic version, the search form is defined by adding <form></form> element to your web page. The form will send an HTTP GET request to the same page that rendered the search form. You can control this behavior by adding additional information to the <form> element. If you want to change the destination, you can add an action attribute to the <form> element. Seeing as we want to remain on this page, we can omit the action attribute.

You will also notice that we are adding a method attribute to this form. This tells the page that we are doing a GET request, and this will always be true when we are searching. If we wanted to modify data, we would use method="post" on the form, but this is not something we would ever want to do in a search form. After adding your <form> markup to your List.cshtml page, the markup should look as illustrated in Code Listing 2-4.

Listing 2-4. Adding the Form to the List.cshtml Page

```
@page
@model VideoStore.Pages.Videos.ListModel
@{
}

<h1>@Model.PageTitle</h1>

<form method="get">
    <div class="form-group">
        <div class="input-group">
            <input type="search" class="form-control" value="" />
            <button class="btn btn-group">
                <i class="fas fa-search"></i>
            </button>
        </div>
    </div>
</form>
```

```
<div class="container-fluid">
    <div class="row">
        <div class="col-md-4">
            Title
        </div>
        <div class="col-md-4">
            Release Date
        </div>
        <div class="col-md-4">
            Genre
        </div>
    </div>
    @foreach (var video in Model.Videos)
    {
        <div class="row">
            <div class="col-md-4">
                @video.Title
            </div>
            <div class="col-md-4">
                @video.ReleaseDate.ToShortDateString()
            </div>
            <div class="col-md-4">
                @video.Genre
            </div>
        </div>
    }
</div>
```

Running your web application, you will see that the search form (Figure 2-1) is rendered above the movie list and that the Font Awesome icon is displayed next to the text input.

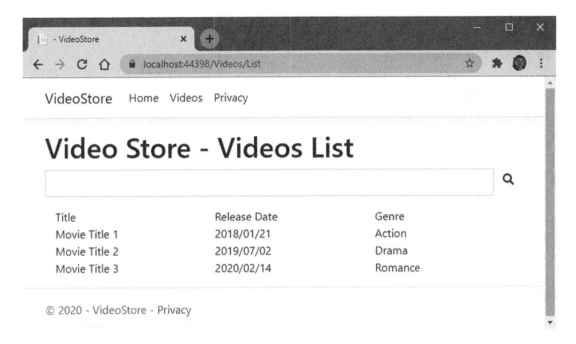

Figure 2-1. *The Search Form*

The next task that we need to do is to add in logic to find videos based on a search term that we enter into the text input. Let's start on that next.

Implementing the Find Logic

For us to implement a search term on the find input, we need to modify our data service slightly. We want to pass the data service a string value for the title that the user of the web page wants to search for. This means that we need to start with the IVideoData Interface.

We want to tell that whatever data service implements this Interface, it should allow for the passing of a string value in the ListVideos method as seen in Code Listing 2-5.

Listing 2-5. The Modified IVideoData Interface

```
namespace VideoStore.Data
{
    public interface IVideoData
    {
        IEnumerable<Video> ListVideos(string title);
    }
}
```

If we modify the Interface, we need to apply that change to the classes that implement that Interface. Swing over to the `TestData` class, and change the `ListVideos` method as illustrated in Code Listing 2-6.

Listing 2-6. The Modified TestData Method

```
public IEnumerable<Video> ListVideos(string title = null) => _videoList
            .Where(x => string.IsNullOrEmpty(title)
            || x.Title.StartsWith(title))
            .OrderBy(x => x.Title);
```

You can see that the title parameter has been made optional. This means that we need to cater for a null string value in the `Where` clause. I have also added more suitable movie names to our test data. With that, the complete TestData class now looks as illustrated in Code Listing 2-7.

Listing 2-7. The TestData Class

```
namespace VideoStore.Data
{
    public class TestData : IVideoData
    {
        List<Video> _videoList;
        public TestData()
        {
            _videoList = new List<Video>()
            {
```

```
            new Video { Id = 1, Title = "Sound of the Seven Seas",
            ReleaseDate = new DateTime(2018, 1, 21), Genre =
            MovieGenre.Action },
            new Video { Id = 2, Title = "A Day in the Sun", ReleaseDate
            = new DateTime(2019, 7, 2), Genre = MovieGenre.Drama },
            new Video { Id = 3, Title = "Wonders of the Universe",
            ReleaseDate = new DateTime(2020, 2, 14), Genre =
            MovieGenre.Romance }
        };
    }
    public IEnumerable<Video> ListVideos(string title = null) => _videoList
        .Where(x => string.IsNullOrEmpty(title)
        || x.Title.StartsWith(title))
        .OrderBy(x => x.Title);
    }
}
```

The last bit we need to do to hook it all up is to tell the search form about this search query that might be entered into the search form. We do this via the name attribute on the input element. So swing back to the List.cshtml file, and modify the <form> element as illustrated in Code Listing 2-8.

Listing 2-8. The Modified Search Form

```
<form method="get">
    <div class="form-group">
        <div class="input-group">
            <input type="search"
                    class="form-control"
                    value=""
                    name="searchQuery"/>
            <button class="btn btn-group">
                <i class="fas fa-search"></i>
            </button>
        </div>
    </div>
</form>
```

You will notice that I have added name="searchQuery" to the input element. The last section of code that we need to modify is the OnGet method of the List.cshtml.cs file as illustrated in Code Listing 2-9.

Listing 2-9. Modified OnGet Method

```
public void OnGet(string searchQuery)
{
    PageTitle = _config["VideoListPageTitle"];
    Videos = _videoData.ListVideos(searchQuery);
}
```

It is interesting to note that the string parameter name, passed to the OnGet method, must match the value in the name attribute of the input element in Code Listing 2-8. This means that if I specify name="searchQuery" in the search form, I then also need to specify public void OnGet(string searchQuery) in the cs file.

Through something we call model binding, ASP.NET Core will have a look at the parameter name in the OnGet method. It will then go out and try to find something named (in our case) searchQuery in the posted form values, in the query string as well as in the HTTP headers. It then passes this value through to our _videoData.ListVideos data service method. If it doesn't find a value for searchQuery, ASP.NET Core will simply pass through a null.

Using Model Binding and Tag Helpers

Let's have a look at how model binding can help us with making the code a bit easier to work with. Whenever the OnGet method is called, it is as a result of the user clicking the link to the page. The page simply does an HTTP GET request.

When the user provides a search query (refer to Listing 2-10), this is considered an input model because it's a value that the user is providing to the page. One can therefore safely say that the properties for PageTitle and Videos are considered output models.

Listing 2-10. The List.cshtml.cs Page

```
public class ListModel : PageModel
{
    private readonly IConfiguration _config;
    private readonly IVideoData _videoData;

    public string PageTitle { get; set; }
    public IEnumerable<Video> Videos { get; set; }

    public ListModel(IConfiguration config, IVideoData videoData)
    {
        _config = config;
        _videoData = videoData;
    }
    public void OnGet(string searchQuery)
    {
        PageTitle = _config["VideoListPageTitle"];
        Videos = _videoData.ListVideos(searchQuery);
    }
}
```

The output models allow me to bind to the returned data, in, for example, a foreach loop as seen in Code Listing 2-4. Taking a closer look at the markup for the form (Listing 2-11), you will notice that the value property is empty.

Listing 2-11. The Search Form Markup

```
<form method="get">
    <div class="form-group">
        <div class="input-group">
            <input type="search"
                   class="form-control"
                   value=""
                   name="searchQuery"/>
            <button class="btn btn-group">
                <i class="fas fa-search"></i>
            </button>
```

```
        </div>
    </div>
</form>
```

What this means is that whenever the user types in a search query (Figure 2-2), the text input will be cleared because the `value` property is not set. Model binding can help us here.

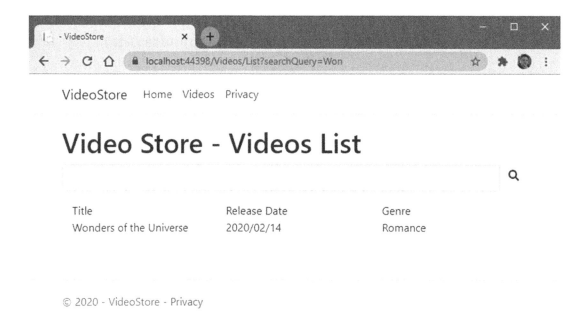

Figure 2-2. *Videos Returned from Search Term*

What if I could have a property on the page that acts as an input and an output model? Something that will accept data as well as display data to the page. As it turns out, there is a special attribute you can use to control this. We will need to change the code for our Video List page slightly. These are the changes that we need to make:

- Add a using statement for Microsoft.AspNetCore.Mvc.

- Create a property called `SearchQuery`, and add an attribute called BindProperty with the BinderType parameter of `SupportsGet` set to `true`.

- Change the `OnGet` method and remove the `searchQuery` parameter and pass the `SearchQuery` property through, instead, to the data service.

The code for the Video List page will now look as in Code Listing 2-12.

Listing 2-12. The Modified List.cshtml.cs Page

```
using Microsoft.AspNetCore.Mvc;
using Microsoft.AspNetCore.Mvc.RazorPages;
using Microsoft.Extensions.Configuration;
using System.Collections.Generic;
using VideoStore.Core;
using VideoStore.Data;

namespace VideoStore.Pages.Videos
{
    public class ListModel : PageModel
    {
        private readonly IConfiguration _config;
        private readonly IVideoData _videoData;

        public string PageTitle { get; set; }
        public IEnumerable<Video> Videos { get; set; }

        [BindProperty(SupportsGet = true)]
        public string SearchQuery { get; set; }

        public ListModel(IConfiguration config, IVideoData videoData)
        {
            _config = config;
            _videoData = videoData;
        }
        public void OnGet()
        {
            PageTitle = _config["VideoListPageTitle"];
            Videos = _videoData.ListVideos(SearchQuery);
        }
    }
}
```

Looking at the `SearchQuery` property, you will notice the attribute called `BindProperty` that has been added. This tells ASP.NET Core that the `SearchQuery` property must act as an input and an output model. This means that whenever the page processes an HTTP request, the `SearchQuery` property will be given information from that request.

The default action of ASP.NET Core is to bind information to the `SearchQuery` property on an HTTP POST operation. Our page is not, however, doing a POST, but a GET. We must therefore tell it to bind information to the `SearchQuery` property during a GET operation.

Adding `SupportsGet = true` to the `BindProperty` attribute does just that. This leaves us with one last thing to do, and that is to modify the `<form>` markup.

Listing 2-13. The Modified Form Markup

```
<form method="get">
    <div class="form-group">
        <div class="input-group">
            <input type="search"
                    class="form-control"
                    asp-for="SearchQuery"/>
            <button class="btn btn-group">
                <i class="fas fa-search"></i>
            </button>
        </div>
    </div>
</form>
```

As illustrated in Code Listing 2-13, the properties for `name` and `value` on the `<input>` element have been replaced with a tag helper called `asp-for`. This tag helper works with ASP.NET Core and model binding. The `asp-for` tag helper is telling the page that the text being entered into this input is for the property `SearchQuery`.

It is important to note that the tag helper already assumes that I am working with an instance of my `ListModel` page. It is for this reason that I can reference the `SearchQuery` property without prefixing it with `Model`.

My ListModel also inherits from the abstract class PageModel. You can see this in the class definition public class ListModel : PageModel in the List.cshtml.cs page. It is for this reason that you can see all the properties (Figure 2-3) of the PageModel class in the asp-for tag helper.

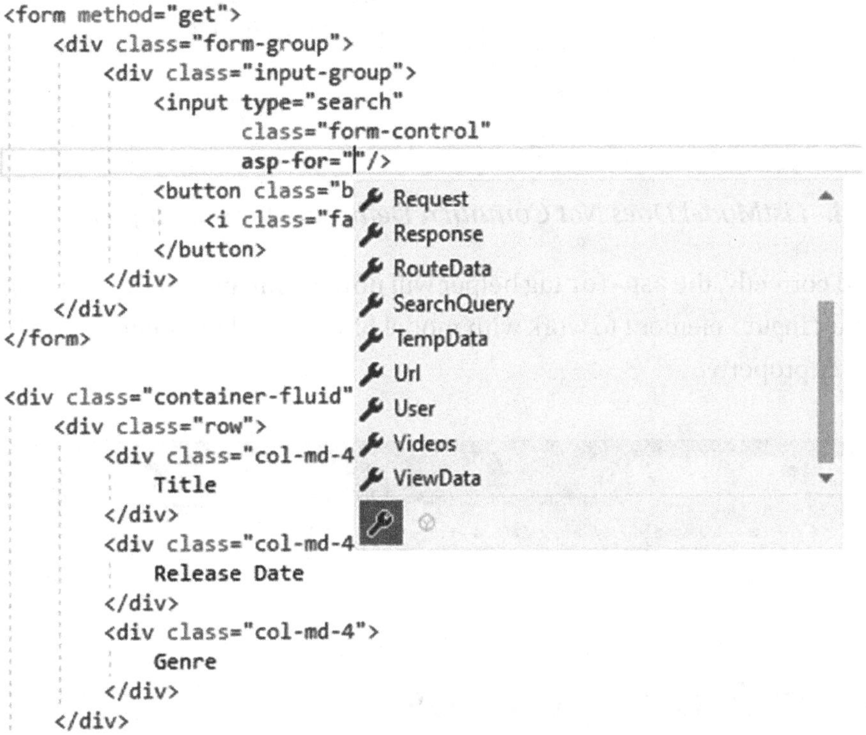

```
<form method="get">
    <div class="form-group">
        <div class="input-group">
            <input type="search"
                   class="form-control"
                   asp-for="|"/>
            <button class="b     Request
                <i class="fa     Response
            </button>            RouteData
        </div>                   SearchQuery
    </div>                       TempData
</form>                          Url

<div class="container-fluid"    User
    <div class="row">           Videos
        <div class="col-md-4    ViewData
            Title
        </div>
        <div class="col-md-4
            Release Date
        </div>
        <div class="col-md-4">
            Genre
        </div>
    </div>
```

Figure 2-3. *The PageModel Properties*

This means that if you don't provide the correct casing for the property (or property that does not exist) in the tag helper, you will get an error as shown in Figure 2-4.

To dig a little deeper into the PageModel class, simply F12 on the class name in the List.cshtml.cs page. There you will see the properties illustrated in Figure 2-4.

You can therefore assume that asp-for knows about your ListModel and the properties it exposes.

```
<form method="get">
    <div class="form-group">
        <div class="input-group">
            <input type="search"
                    class="form-control"
                    asp-for="searchquery"/>
            <button class="btn btn-group">
                <i class="fas fa-search"></i>
            </button>
        </div>
    </div>
</form>
```

Figure 2-4. *ListModel Does Not Contain a Definition for searchquery*

Spelled correctly, the `asp-for` tag helper will now go out and set the name and value of the `<input>` element to work with model binding and populate the value of the SearchQuery property.

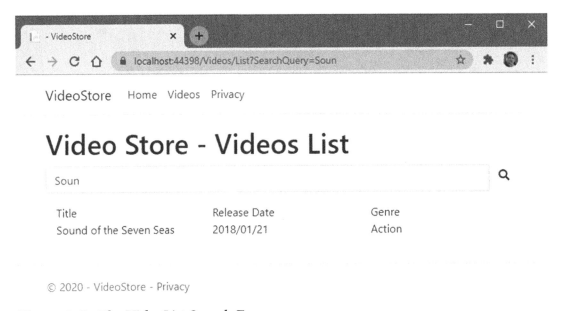

Figure 2-5. *The VideoList Search Form*

I am now able to search for a specific video in my list of videos and, after I click the search button, see the value I searched for in the input (Figure 2-5).

Displaying Related Data

Having a list of videos is great, but ideally, you would want to view more information about a specific video. Displaying related data like this is a great case for using a detail page.

With a detail page, you can send the user off to a part of the site that will display detailed information regarding the specific video you clicked on. To start, in the Solution Explorer, right-click the Videos folder under Pages and add a new Razor page.

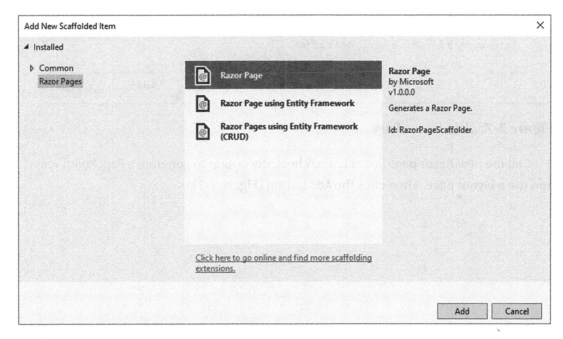

Figure 2-6. *Add New Scaffolded Item*

You will see the Add New Scaffolded Item screen (Figure 2-6). Just select to add a Razor Page.

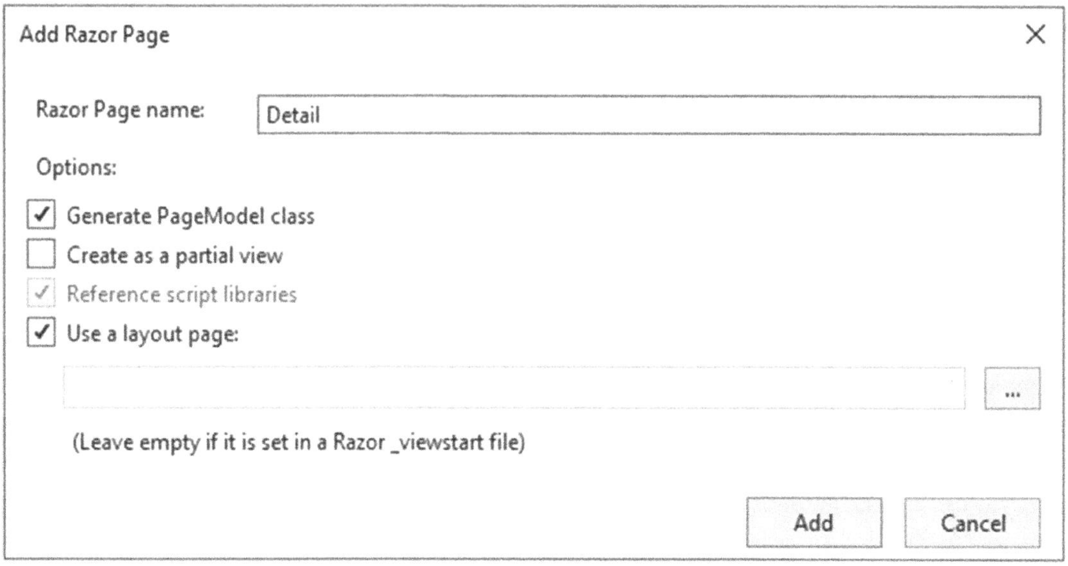

Figure 2-7. *Add Razor Page*

Call the new Razor page Detail, and check the option to generate a PageModel class and use a layout page. Then click the Add button (Figure 2-7).

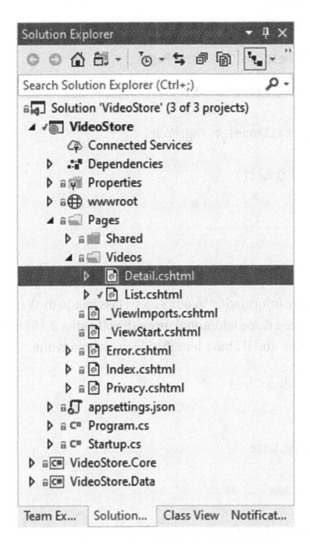

Figure 2-8. *The Solution Explorer After Adding the Detail Page*

Once the Detail page has been added, your Solution Explorer will look as in Figure 2-8. Having a look at the DetailModel class, you will see the boilerplate code (Figure 2-14) that we will be modifying next to display the video details.

Listing 2-14. The DetailModel Class

```
using Microsoft.AspNetCore.Mvc.RazorPages;

namespace VideoStore.Pages.Videos
{
    public class DetailModel : PageModel
    {
        public void OnGet()
        {

        }
    }
}
```

First, let's add more information to our Video class inside the VideoStore.Core project. I have just added three additional properties (Listing 2-15) that will help me see what I paid for the video and if I have lent the video out to anyone.

Listing 2-15. The Video Class

```
using System;

namespace VideoStore.Core
{
    public class Video
    {
        public int Id { get; set; }
        public string Title { get; set; }
        public DateTime ReleaseDate { get; set; }
        public MovieGenre Genre { get; set; }
        public double Price { get; set; }
        public bool LentOut { get; set; }
        public string LentTo { get; set; }
    }
}
```

I then need to add more test data for these properties to the TestData services' constructor in the VideoStore.Data project (Listing 2-16).

Listing 2-16. The Added Test Data

```
public TestData()
{
    _videoList = new List<Video>()
    {
        new Video { Id = 1, Title = "Sound of the Seven Seas", ReleaseDate
        = new DateTime(2018, 1, 21), Genre = MovieGenre.Action, Price =
        5.99, LentOut = false, LentTo = "" },
        new Video { Id = 2, Title = "A Day in the Sun", ReleaseDate = new
        DateTime(2019, 7, 2), Genre = MovieGenre.Drama, Price = 4.59,
        LentOut = false, LentTo = "" },
        new Video { Id = 3, Title = "Wonders of the Universe", ReleaseDate
        = new DateTime(2020, 2, 14), Genre = MovieGenre.Romance, Price =
        12.99, LentOut = true, LentTo = "Joah Sanderson" }
    };
}
```

Once I have more video details added, I can go ahead and build out the Detail page with more information. Start by adding a using statement to bring in the VideoStore. Core namespace. Then add a property for Video to the DetailModel class (Listing 2-17).

Listing 2-17. The Modified DetailModel Class

```
using Microsoft.AspNetCore.Mvc.RazorPages;
using VideoStore.Core;

namespace VideoStore.Pages.Videos
{
    public class DetailModel : PageModel
    {
        public Video Video { get; set; }

        public void OnGet()
        {

        }
    }
}
```

We can now turn our attention to the Detail.cshtml markup as illustrated in Code Listing 2-18.

Listing 2-18. The Detail Page Markup

```
@page
@model VideoStore.Pages.Videos.DetailModel
@{
    ViewData["Title"] = "Detail";
}

<h1>Detail</h1>
```

Add some more detail to the markup as illustrated in Code Listing 2-19. Here, we can simply add a series of div elements to hold the various Video properties. You will also notice that I used an HTML Helper for the check box to check the check box if the video is lent out to anyone. I also only display the LentTo property value if the LentOut property is true.

Listing 2-19. The Expanded Detail Markup

```
@page
@model VideoStore.Pages.Videos.DetailModel
@{
    ViewData["Title"] = "Detail";
}

<h1>@Model.Video.Title</h1>

<div>
    Catalog ID: @Model.Video.Id
</div>
<div>
    Release Date: @Model.Video.ReleaseDate.ToString("dd MMMM yyyy")
</div>
<div>
    Genre: @Model.Video.Genre
</div>
```

```
<div>
    Price: $@Model.Video.Price
</div>
<div>
    Lent Out: @Html.CheckBoxFor(x => x.Video.LentOut)
</div>

@if (Model.Video.LentOut == true)
{
    <div>
        Lent To: @Model.Video.LentTo
    </div>
}

<a asp-page="./List" class="btn btn-outline-primary">Back to Videos</a>
```

Lastly, I add a way to go back to the Video List page by using the asp-page tag helper. This tag helper will look for a page in the current directory, which is the Videos directory, called List.

Passing the Video ID Through to the Detail Page

With our Detail page containing the elements to display the video details, we need to pass the ID of a selected video through from our List page to our Detail page.

We can do this by modifying the DetailModel class slightly as seen in Code Listing 2-20. It's as simple as giving the OnGet method an Integer parameter for the Video ID and setting it to the Video.Id property.

Listing 2-20. Passing a Video ID to the DetailModel Class

```
using Microsoft.AspNetCore.Mvc.RazorPages;
using VideoStore.Core;

namespace VideoStore.Pages.Videos
{
    public class DetailModel : PageModel
    {
        public Video Video { get; set; }
```

```
        public void OnGet(int videoId)
        {
            Video = new Video();
            Video.Id = videoId;
        }
    }
}
```

Moving back to the markup for the List.cshtml page, we must now modify it slightly to get the video ID and pass it through to the Detail page whenever a user clicks a video. For this, we will add a column that contains a button that the user can click to navigate to the Detail page.

If you think back to the code in Listing 2-4, you will remember that we just wrote the markup to display the videos on the page.

Listing 2-21. The Modified List.cshtml Page

```
<div class="container-fluid">
    <div class="row">
        <div class="col-md-3">
            Title
        </div>
        <div class="col-md-3">
            Release Date
        </div>
        <div class="col-md-3">
            Genre
        </div>
        <div class="col-md-3">

        </div>
    </div>
    @foreach (var video in Model.Videos)
    {
        <div class="row">
            <div class="col-md-3">
                @video.Title
```

```
        </div>
        <div class="col-md-3">
            @video.ReleaseDate.ToShortDateString()
        </div>
        <div class="col-md-3">
            @video.Genre
        </div>
        <div class="col-md-3">
            <div>
                <a class="btn btn-lg" asp-page="./Detail" asp-route-
                videoId="@video.Id">
                    <i class="fas fa-info-circle"></i>
                </a>
            </div>
        </div>
    </div>
    }
</div>
```

Modify the markup as illustrated in Code Listing 2-21 to add a div element to contain a button that the user can click to navigate to the Detail page.

Please note that I have not included the full markup for the List.cshtml page in Listing 2-21. The complete source code is available on GitHub.

Let's take a closer look at the tag helpers on the <a> link element. To make it easier, I have added just the button code to the code in Listing 2-22.

Listing 2-22. The Button Tag Helpers

```
<div class="col-md-3">
    <div>
        <a class="btn btn-lg" asp-page="./Detail" asp-route-videoId="@video.Id">
            <i class="fas fa-info-circle"></i>
        </a>
    </div>
</div>
```

You can see that we are using the same tag helper, `asp-page`, that we previously used in Listings 2-1 and 2-19 to specify a page to navigate to (which is the Detail page in this example). It does this by setting the `href` attribute to point to the correct page.

Tag helpers are the preferred way to add logic to your page because they know about the structure and inputs that the page needs. Tag helpers are therefore flexible because if you change your page in any way, the tag helpers will automatically know about that change. In addition to telling the tag helpers which page we need to navigate to, we also need a way to pass the video ID to the Detail page. This is where the `asp-route` tag helper comes in handy. It is a little more dynamic and allows me to include the parameter name that I want to pass to the Detail page by including it in the tag helper name.

This means that when I write `asp-route-videoId` and give it the video ID as a parameter value, the tag helper will figure out how to pass the video ID to the Detail page.

```
▼ <div class="col-md-3">
  ▼ <div>
    ▼ <a class="btn btn-lg" href="/Videos/Detail?videoId=1">
      ▶ <i class="fas fa-info-circle" aria-hidden="true">…</i>
      </a>
    </div>
  </div>
```

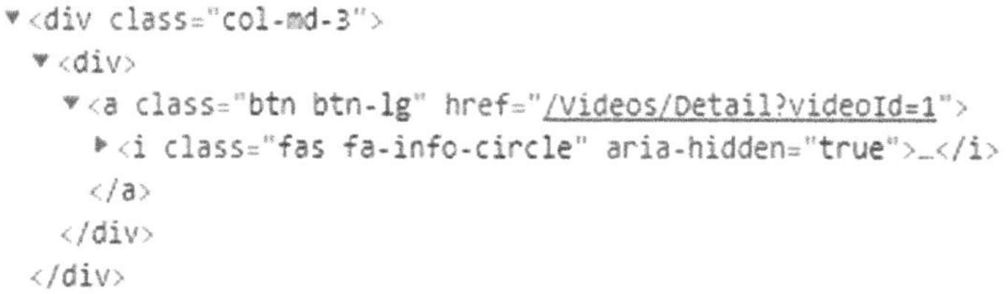

Figure 2-9. *The Generated HTML for Code Listing 2-22*

Referring back to the code in Listing 2-22 and taking a look at the rendered code in Figure 2-9, you can see how the tag helpers rendered the markup based on one of the videos on our list. The `href` value has been populated with the use of tag helpers and will navigate the user to the Detail page, passing that page the specific video ID.

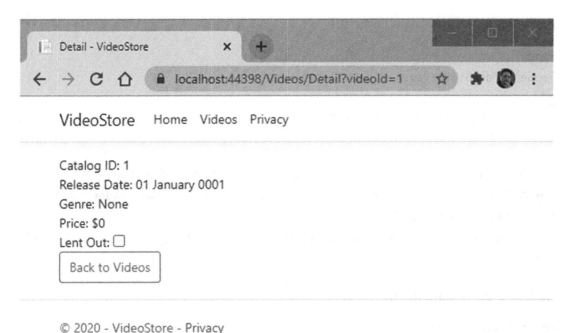

Figure 2-10. *The Video Detail Page*

If we click a video in the list, then the ID of that video will be passed to the Detail page as seen in Figure 2-10. The URL to that page is also as we expected (Listing 2-23) where the video ID is being passed to the Detail page in the query string.

Listing 2-23. The URL to the Detail Page

```
https://localhost:44398/Videos/Detail?videoId=1
```

ASP.NET Core allows us to control this behavior with page routes. We don't have to stick with the URL format, using a query string, generated by the tag helpers. Let's have a look at how to control this behavior.

Working with Page Routes

A common way for web pages to pass values to other pages is to make use of the URL path. I don't have to use the query string to pass the video ID through to the Detail page. I can control this behavior by modifying the @page directive in the Detail.cshtml page. Referring back to the code in Listing 2-19, you will see the @page directive, illustrated in Listing 2-24, at the top of the page.

Listing 2-24. The @page Directive

```
@page
@model VideoStore.Pages.Videos.DetailModel
@{
    ViewData["Title"] = "Detail";
}
```

Here, I can supply ASP.NET Core a string parameter after the @page directive, telling it what I want the route to be. Remember, the URL will always start with /Videos/Detail as illustrated in Listing 2-23.

If I specify a different route in the @page directive, I can change the URL as illustrated in Listing 2-25.

Listing 2-25. Changing the Route

```
@page "/Videos/Store"
@model VideoStore.Pages.Videos.DetailModel
@{
    ViewData["Title"] = "Detail";
}
```

If I run the web application and navigate to the Detail page for a specific video, I see that my URL has changed as illustrated in Figure 2-11.

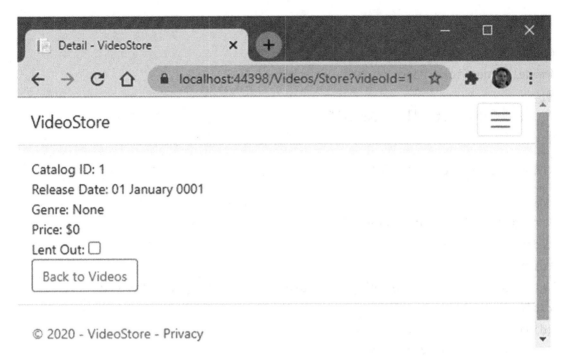

Figure 2-11. *The Changed URL*

This still contains the query string though, and what I want to do is introduce a new URL segment containing the video ID parameter. I can do this by adding the parameter inside of curly braces as seen in Listing 2-26.

Listing 2-26. The Video ID as a New URL Segment

```
@page "{videoId}"
@model VideoStore.Pages.Videos.DetailModel
@{
    ViewData["Title"] = "Detail";
}
```

This tells ASP.NET Core that I want my page URL to be Videos/Detail/{videoId} where {videoId} is the ID of the video clicked in the list of videos. This {videoId} can be further constrained by specifying the data type "{videoId:int}". Here, I am telling ASP. NET Core that the ID parameter must be an Integer value.

With this in place, the complete code for the Detail.cshtml page will be as illustrated in Code Listing 2-27.

Listing 2-27. Complete Code Listing for the Detail.cshtml Page

```
@page "{videoId:int}"
@model VideoStore.Pages.Videos.DetailModel
@{
    ViewData["Title"] = "Detail";
}

<h1>@Model.Video.Title</h1>

<div>
    Catalog ID: @Model.Video.Id
</div>
<div>
    Release Date: @Model.Video.ReleaseDate.ToString("dd MMMM yyyy")
</div>
<div>
    Genre: @Model.Video.Genre
</div>
<div>
    Price: $@Model.Video.Price
</div>
<div>
    Lent Out: @Html.CheckBoxFor(x => x.Video.LentOut)
</div>

@if (Model.Video.LentOut == true)
{
    <div>
        Lent To: @Model.Video.LentTo
    </div>
}

<a asp-page="./List" class="btn btn-outline-primary">Back to Videos</a>
```

Running the web application, the URL is now exactly as I want it to be (Figure 2-12). If I wanted to tell ASP.NET that the ID parameter is optional, I could also have specified this in the @page directive by specifying "{videoId?:int}". Whatever I do here though,

ASP.NET Core knows that the third segment of the URL will specify a parameter called videoId.

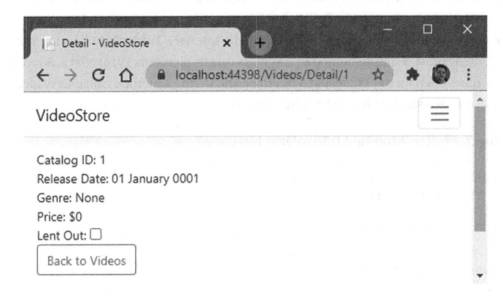

Figure 2-12. *The Correct URL Format*

If we compare the image in Figure 2-9 with the image in Figure 2-13, you will notice how the tag helpers have changed the markup. It now specifies a new URL segment.

```
▼ <div class="col-md-3">
  ▼ <div>
    ▼ <a class="btn btn-lg" href="/Videos/Detail/1">
      ▶ <i class="fas fa-info-circle" aria-hidden="true">_</i>
      </a>
    </div>
  </div>
```

Figure 2-13. *The Generated Markup Specifying the ID in the Page Route*

All we have done here is pass the Video ID through to the Detail page. As you can see, none of the other details have been displayed on the Detail page at all, and this is expected. If you look back at the code in Listing 2-20, you will see that we are only setting the Video.Id property.

Populating Video Details

To populate the Detail page with the specific video data, we need to make a few small changes. We need to modify the TestData class to return a video by ID. It is at this point that you should be thinking of modifying the Interface IVideoData because this functionality must be implemented by any class that implements IVideoData. So with this in mind, open up the IVideoData Interface and define a method called GetVideo that will return a single video by ID (Listing 2-28).

Listing 2-28. The Modified IVideoData Interface

```
using System.Collections.Generic;
using VideoStore.Core;

namespace VideoStore.Data
{
    public interface IVideoData
    {
        IEnumerable<Video> ListVideos(string title);
        Video GetVideo(int id);
    }
}
```

As you know, because we have modified our Interface, we also need to implement that change on the TestData class that implements the IVideoData Interface.

Listing 2-29. The Complete TestData Class

```
using System;
using System.Collections.Generic;
using System.Linq;
using VideoStore.Core;

namespace VideoStore.Data
{
    public class TestData : IVideoData
    {
        List<Video> _videoList;
```

```
public TestData()
{
    _videoList = new List<Video>()
    {
        new Video { Id = 1, Title = "Sound of the Seven Seas",
        ReleaseDate = new DateTime(2018, 1, 21), Genre =
        MovieGenre.Action, Price = 5.99, LentOut = false, LentTo =
        "" },
        new Video { Id = 2, Title = "A Day in the Sun", ReleaseDate
        = new DateTime(2019, 7, 2), Genre = MovieGenre.Drama, Price
        = 4.59, LentOut = false, LentTo = "" },
        new Video { Id = 3, Title = "Wonders of the Universe",
        ReleaseDate = new DateTime(2020, 2, 14), Genre =
        MovieGenre.Romance, Price = 12.99, LentOut = true, LentTo =
        "Joah Sanderson" }
    };
}
public IEnumerable<Video> ListVideos(string title = null) => _
videoList
    .Where(x => string.IsNullOrEmpty(title)
    || x.Title.StartsWith(title))
    .OrderBy(x => x.Title);

public Video GetVideo(int id) => _videoList.SingleOrDefault(x =>
x.Id == id);
    }
}
```

The expression-bodied GetVideo method in Listing 2-29 simply returns a video from the _videoList collection. This now matches the Interface definition. The last section of code that we need to modify is on our Detail.cshtml.cs page.

You will need to add a reference to the VideoStore.Data namespace in the using statements of the Detail.cshtml.cs class.

With the relevant namespace added, modify the Detail.cshtml.cs page as illustrated in Listing 2-30.

Listing 2-30. The Modified Detail Page

```
using Microsoft.AspNetCore.Mvc.RazorPages;
using VideoStore.Core;
using VideoStore.Data;

namespace VideoStore.Pages.Videos
{
    public class DetailModel : PageModel
    {
        private readonly IVideoData _videoData;

        public Video Video { get; set; }

        public DetailModel(IVideoData videoData)
        {
            _videoData = videoData;
        }
        public void OnGet(int videoId)
        {
            Video = _videoData.GetVideo(videoId);
        }
    }
}
```

I have simply added a constructor to the page that accepts an object of type IVideoData which is then initialized to a private field _videoData.

I like naming my private fields with a leading underscore. Some developers keep the field name and the parameter name the same, prefixing the private field with the `this` keyword. For me, an underscore `_videoData = videoData` is cleaner than `this.videoData = videoData`.

In the OnGet method, I can change the code to use the data service to get a specific video. This is all we need to do. Go ahead and run your application.

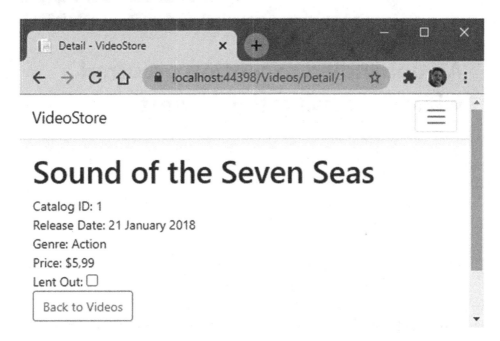

Figure 2-14. *The Video Detail Page*

When you click one of the videos in the list, the video ID is passed through to the Detail page, and the video details are populated as seen in Figure 2-14. The last bit of work that we would need to do is to handle any bad requests coming to our Detail page. In the image in Figure 2-14, you will notice (in the URL) that the video ID being passed to the Detail page is ID 1. If the user tried to change this ID to anything other than what our video collection contains, a null reference exception would occur. Let's fix that in the next section.

Handling Bad Requests

At some point in time, you might need to handle bad requests. Assume that the user accidentally typed in the incorrect URL, or bookmarked a video that no longer exists in the catalog. Sending the user to the Detail page for a nonexistent ID will result in a NullReferenceException as seen in Figure 2-15.

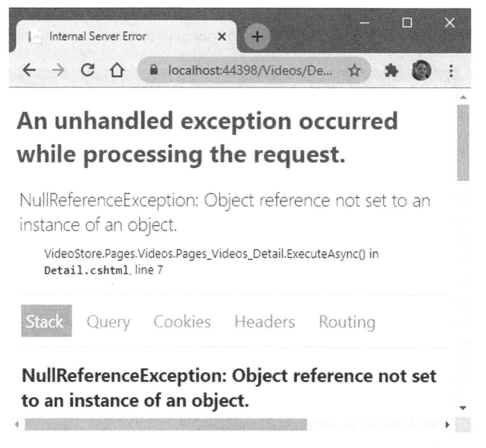

Figure 2-15. *A NullReferenceException Page*

By default, ASP.NET Core projects are created with some boilerplate code in place. This is very convenient. One such section of code is in the `Startup.cs` page, in the `Configure` method. The code that handles exceptions is illustrated in Listing 2-31.

Listing 2-31. Handling Errors

```
if (env.IsDevelopment())
{
    _ = app.UseDeveloperExceptionPage();
}
else
{
    _ = app.UseExceptionHandler("/Error");
    _ = app.UseHsts();
}
```

What this code does is display a developer exception page (Figure 2-15) when you are in development. When your application is not in development mode, the web application will redirect to a generic Error page (Figure 2-16).

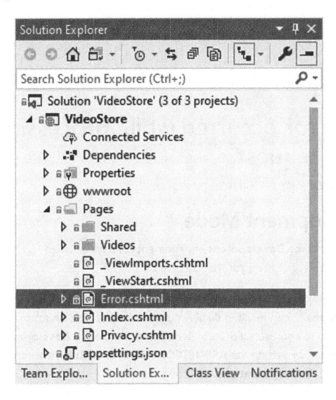

Figure 2-16. *The Error Page*

When this Error page is displayed, the page just informs the user that something went wrong and that Development Mode is required to see specifics.

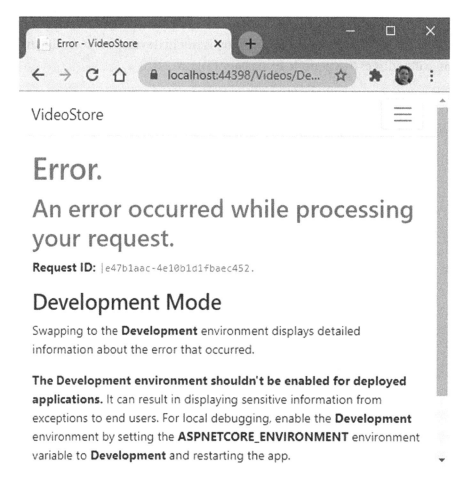

Figure 2-17. *The Generic Error Page*

You never want to show developer exception messages to a user in production. Not only does this create a bad user experience (the impression of a buggy web application) but also poses a security risk.

The Error page in Figure 2-17 is great for unhandled errors in your application, but I would like a bit more control over the errors displayed to the user.

To do this, add another Razor page to the Videos folder called VideoError as seen in Figure 2-18.

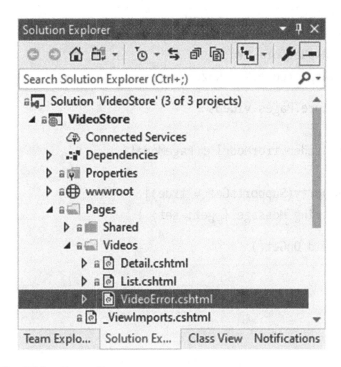

Figure 2-18. *The VideoError Page*

Thinking back to the section on working with page routes, add a `message` parameter to the @page directive (Listing 2-32).

Listing 2-32. The VideoError Markup

```
@page "{message}"
@model VideoStore.Pages.Videos.VideoErrorModel
@{
    ViewData["Title"] = "VideoError";
}

<h1>Error</h1>

<div>@Model.Message</div>

<a asp-page="./List" class="btn alert-info">Back to Video List</a>
```

The @Model.Message property does not exist yet, but we'll add that next. On the VideoError.cshtml.cs page, add the code in Listing 2-33.

Listing 2-33. The VideoErrorModel Class

```
using Microsoft.AspNetCore.Mvc;
using Microsoft.AspNetCore.Mvc.RazorPages;

namespace VideoStore.Pages.Videos
{
    public class VideoErrorModel : PageModel
    {
        [BindProperty(SupportsGet = true)]
        public string Message { get; set; }

        public void OnGet()
        {

        }
    }
}
```

This code should feel very familiar to you. It's the same logic we used in the List. cshtml.cs page. You will notice the BindProperty attribute on the Message property. This tells ASP.NET Core that the Message property must act as an input and an output model. This means that whenever the page processes an HTTP request, the Message property will be given information from that request. The last change we need to make is to the Detail.cshtml.cs page as illustrated in Listing 2-34.

Listing 2-34. The DetailModel with the Modified OnGet Method

```
using Microsoft.AspNetCore.Mvc;
using Microsoft.AspNetCore.Mvc.RazorPages;
using VideoStore.Core;
using VideoStore.Data;

namespace VideoStore.Pages.Videos
{
    public class DetailModel : PageModel
    {
        private readonly IVideoData _videoData;

        public Video Video { get; set; }
```

```
    public DetailModel(IVideoData videoData)
    {
        _videoData = videoData;
    }

    public IActionResult OnGet(int videoId)
    {
        Video = _videoData.GetVideo(videoId);

        return Video == null ? RedirectToPage("./VideoError", new {
        message = "The video does not exist" }) : (IActionResult)
        Page();
    }
    }
}
```

The OnGet method has changed slightly. It now returns an IActionResult and defines a contract that represents the result of the OnGet method. If the Video object returned is not null, render the page. If the Video object is null, then redirect to the VideoError page and pass it the message "The video does not exist". Run your web application and pass it the following URL in Listing 2-35.

Listing 2-35. A Request with an Incorrect Video ID

```
https://localhost:44398/Videos/Detail/10
```

The OnGet method will now redirect to the Error page in Figure 2-19.

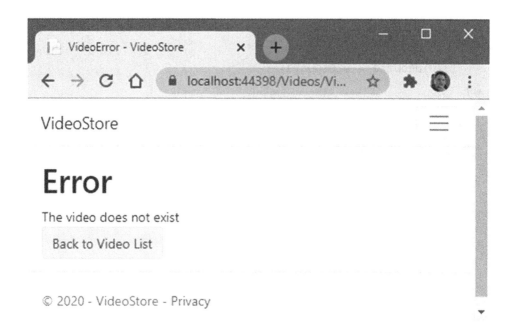

Figure 2-19. *The VideoError Page with Our Message*

The magic of model binding took the message we provided and displayed it on the
VideoError page.

CHAPTER 3

Modifying Data

In the last chapter, we implemented some search logic to find specific videos. We also created a detail page to display the video details after a user clicks a specific video. A logical next step for our application is to be able to modify the data we display.

The logical place to do this would be from the Video List page. Here, the user can click a specific video in the list to view more details about that video or to edit the details of that video. Let's have a look at how to do that in the next sections.

Editing Existing Data and Using Tag Helpers

Having a look at the markup on the Video List page, you will see that the @foreach section builds up the list of videos. It is here, too, that we added logic to create a link to the Detail page.

We can use much of this existing logic to take the user to a page where they can edit the video. The existing markup is illustrated in Listing 3-1.

Listing 3-1. The Existing ForEach Detail Page Markup

```
@foreach (var video in Model.Videos)
{
    <div class="row">
        <div class="col-md-3">
            @video.Title
        </div>
        <div class="col-md-3">
            @video.ReleaseDate.ToShortDateString()
        </div>
        <div class="col-md-3">
            @video.Genre
        </div>
```

© Dirk Strauss 2021
D. Strauss, *Creating ASP.NET Core Web Applications*, https://doi.org/10.1007/978-1-4842-6828-5_3

```
    <div class="col-md-3">
        <div>
            <a class="btn btn-lg" asp-page="./Detail" asp-route-
            videoId="@video.Id">
                <i class="fas fa-info-circle"></i>
            </a>
        </div>
    </div>
  </div>
}
```

What we want to do is add a second link after the one that takes us to the Detail page. To keep it all neat, I added another div with the row class and moved the div with the link to the Detail page inside there. I then added a link for a new page (which we will create in a minute) called Edit. Refer to the code in Listing 3-2.

Listing 3-2. The Modified ForEach Detail Page Markup

```
@foreach (var video in Model.Videos)
{
    <div class="row">
        <div class="col-md-3">
            @video.Title
        </div>
        <div class="col-md-3">
            @video.ReleaseDate.ToShortDateString()
        </div>
        <div class="col-md-3">
            @video.Genre
        </div>
        <div class="col-md-3">
            <div class="row">
                <div class="col-md-6">
                    <a class="btn btn-lg" asp-page="./Detail" asp-route-
                    videoId="@video.Id">
                        <i class="fas fa-info-circle"></i>
                    </a>
```

```
            </div>
            <div class="col-md-6">
                <a class="btn btn-lg" asp-page="./Edit" asp-route-
                videoId="@video.Id">
                    <i class="fa fa-pencil"></i>
                </a>
            </div>
        </div>
    </div>
</div>
}
```

Running the web application, you should see that the edit button has now been added to the Video List page (Figure 3-1). Currently, it doesn't go anywhere because the Edit page does not exist yet.

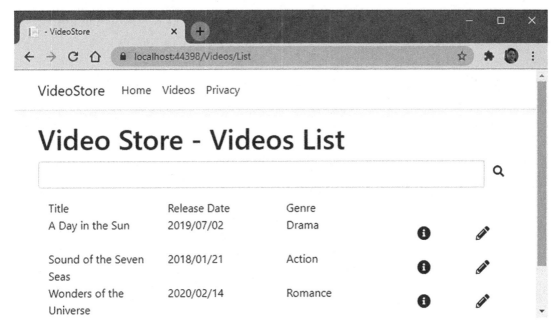

Figure 3-1. *The Video List Page with an Edit Button*

In the Solution Explorer, right-click the Videos folder and add a new Razor page. Name this Razor page Edit, and keep the defaults for the PageModel class and the layout page, and click the Add button (Figure 3-2).

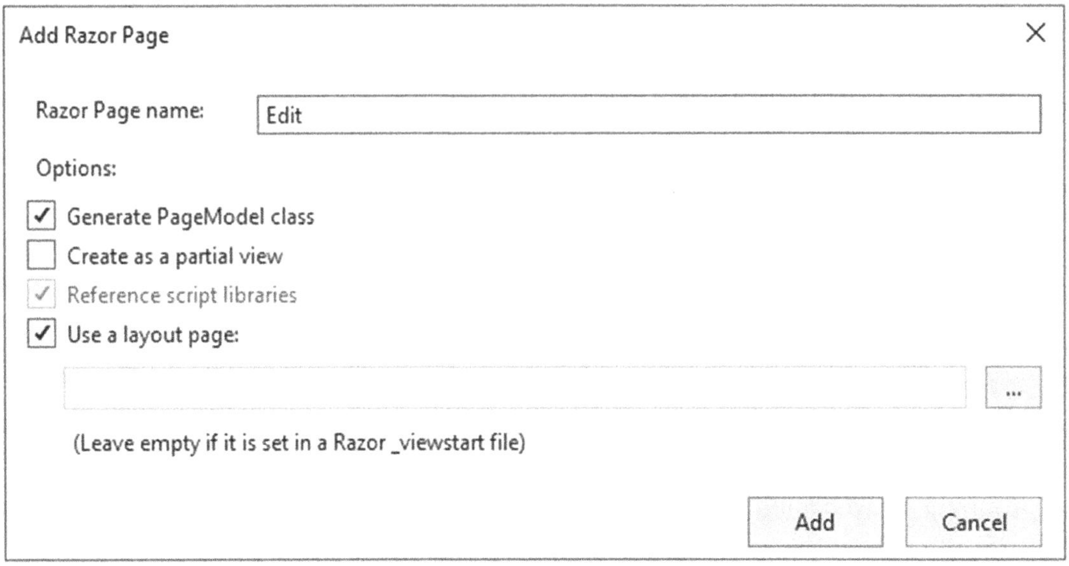

Add Razor Page	✕

Razor Page name: Edit

Options:

☑ Generate PageModel class
☐ Create as a partial view
☑ Reference script libraries
☑ Use a layout page:

[   ] [...]

(Leave empty if it is set in a Razor _viewstart file)

[Add]   [Cancel]

Figure 3-2. *Adding the Edit Page*

Once the Edit page has been added to your solution, your Videos folder should look as illustrated in Figure 3-3.

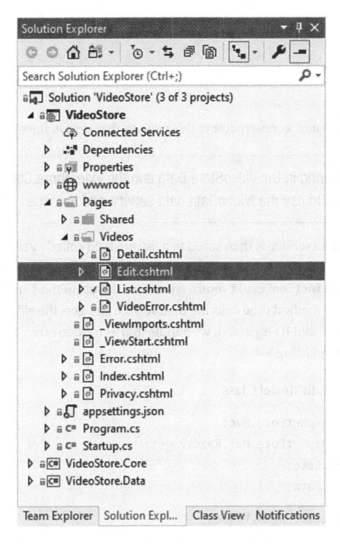

Figure 3-3. *The Added Edit Page in the Solution Explorer*

Having a look at the Edit.cshtml.cs page, you will recognize the boilerplate code (Listing 3-3) that has been added for us.

Listing 3-3. The Edit Page Boilerplate Code

```
namespace VideoStore.Pages.Videos
{
    public class EditModel : PageModel
    {
        public void OnGet()
```

```
        {

        }

    }

}
```

We now need to add a constructor to this page so that we can inject our data service.

You will need to bring in the VideoStore.Data and the VideoStore.Core namespaces before being able to use the IVideoData data service and the Video class.

The injected data service is then saved to a private field called _videoData. We then add a property called Video to the EditModel class that will contain the video we want to edit, and add the IActionResult return type to the OnGet method and pass it the videoId. The OnGet method then calls the data service and gets the video data for the supplied ID. If an invalid ID is passed, we handle that as a video error. The complete code is illustrated in Listing 3-4.

Listing 3-4. The EditModel Class

```
using Microsoft.AspNetCore.Mvc;
using Microsoft.AspNetCore.Mvc.RazorPages;
using VideoStore.Core;
using VideoStore.Data;

namespace VideoStore.Pages.Videos
{
    public class EditModel : PageModel
    {
        private readonly IVideoData _videoData;

        public Video Video { get; set; }

        public EditModel(IVideoData videoData)
        {
            _videoData = videoData;
        }
```

```
public IActionResult OnGet(int videoId)
{
    Video = _videoData.GetVideo(videoId);

    return Video == null ? RedirectToPage("./VideoError", new {
    message = "The video does not exist" }) : (IActionResult)
    Page();
}
}
}
```

If this code feels slightly familiar, then it is because it is almost an exact copy of the Detail page. Just like the Detail page, we want to specify the videoId attribute after the @ page directive.

Listing 3-5. The Edit Page Markup

```
@page "{videoId:int}"
@model VideoStore.Pages.Videos.EditModel
@{
    ViewData["Title"] = "Edit";
}

<h1>Editing: @Model.Video.Title</h1>
```

The markup illustrated in Listing 3-5 shows us the modified page. You will also notice that we have added the video title to the <h1> tag.

Running the web application will show the changes we have made to the Video List page (Figure 3-4).

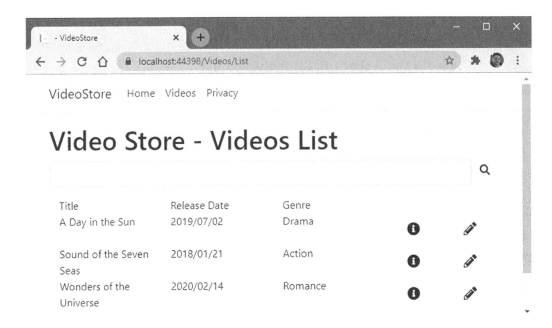

Figure 3-4. *The Modified Video List Page*

Clicking the edit button next to one of the videos in the list will take us to the Edit page (Figure 3-5).

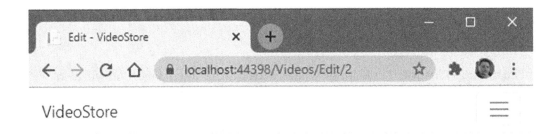

Figure 3-5. *The Edit Page*

Here, you can see that the Edit page is displaying the title of the video we clicked and the URL contains the video ID. Up until now, the creation of the Edit page has been rather straightforward. We now need to start building the Edit page by adding the required controls on the page. Let's do that next.

Building the Edit Form

Thinking back to Chapter 2, you will remember that we added a search form to the List. cshtml page. There, the form method was set as a GET because we were reading data. Now, we want to edit video data, and for that, we need to use a POST.

At its most basic, we will need to add the <form> markup as illustrated in Listing 3-6.

Listing 3-6. The Basic Form with a Post Method

```
<form method="post">
    <button type="submit" class="btn border-primary">Update Video</button>
</form>
```

Using this basic boilerplate code, we now need to add additional <div> elements to add labels and input for the video data. Looking back at the Video class in the VideoStore.Core project, you will see all the properties that you need to add input for. The code in Listing 3-7 is the complete code for the form that we need to edit the video data.

Listing 3-7. Complete Edit Markup

```
@page "{videoId:int}"

@using VideoStore.Core;

@model VideoStore.Pages.Videos.EditModel
@{
    ViewData["Title"] = "Edit";
}

<h1>Editing: @Model.Video.Title</h1>

<form method="post">
```

```
<input type="hidden" asp-for="Video.Id" />
<div class="form-group">
    <label asp-for="Video.Title"></label>
    <input asp-for="Video.Title" class="form-control" />
</div>

<div class="form-group">
    <label asp-for="Video.ReleaseDate"></label>
    <input asp-for="Video.ReleaseDate" class="form-control" />
</div>

<div class="form-group">
    <label asp-for="Video.Genre"></label>
    <select class="form-control" asp-for="Video.Genre"
            asp-items="Html.GetEnumSelectList<MovieGenre>()">
    </select>
</div>

<div class="form-group">
    <label asp-for="Video.Price"></label>
    <input asp-for="Video.Price" class="form-control" />
</div>

<div class="form-group">
    <label asp-for="Video.LentOut"></label>
    <input asp-for="Video.LentOut" class="form-control" />
</div>

<div class="form-group">
    <label asp-for="Video.LentTo"></label>
    <input asp-for="Video.LentTo" class="form-control" />
</div>

<button type="submit" class="btn border-primary">Update Video</button>
</form>
```

I would like to point out a few things here. Underneath the @page directive, you will see that I have imported the VideoStore.Core namespace. This is to allow us to reference the MovieGenre enum in a drop-down list on the form. This code is illustrated in Listing 3-8.

Listing 3-8. The MovieGenre Drop-down

```
<div class="form-group">
    <label asp-for="Video.Genre"></label>
    <select class="form-control" asp-for="Video.Genre"
            asp-items="Html.GetEnumSelectList<MovieGenre>()">
    </select>
</div>
```

For each label and input tag, you will notice that we make use of the asp-for tag helper. By using asp-for, we set the name attribute of the input so that model binding knows what to do with the value supplied. In other words, the asp-for="Video.Title" attribute will know that the value supplied is for the title of the video.

With the MovieGenre, for example, the items in the enum can't be bound to an <input>. We also don't want to allow the user to type in a value, because we need them to select one of the options in the MovieGenre enum.

It is for this reason that we make use of an HTML <select> in the markup. This will generate a drop-down list with the MovieGenre enum values as its items. By using the asp-items tag helper, we can tell it to use a collection of items as its drop-down items by giving it the HTML helper Html.GetEnumSelectList<MovieGenre>().

If we run the web application now, we will see that the drop-down list has been populated with the enum values and that the drop-down has selected the correct video genre (Figure 3-6) for the selected video.

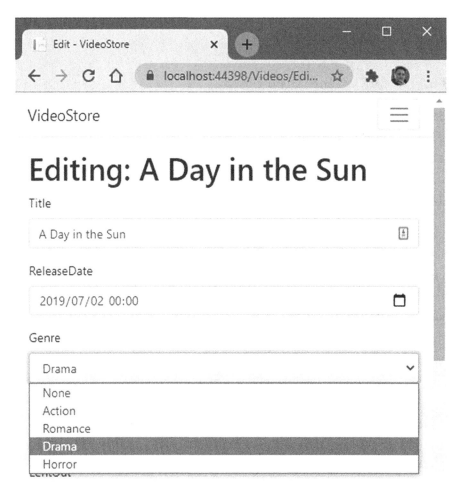

Figure 3-6. *The Edit Form with the Drop-down for Genre*

You could also manually add items to your `<select>` element by adding in `<option>` elements as illustrated in Listing 3-9.

Listing 3-9. Manually Specifying Drop-down Items

```
<select class="form-control" asp-for="Video.Genre">
    <option>Test 1</option>
    <option>Test 2</option>
    <option>Test 3</option>
</select>
```

This is, however, not something that we want to do here. There is another way to bind the dropdown list and that is to add some logic to my EditModel. This removes the need to add a using statement to the Razor page and allows me to specify the items required for the drop-down list in my EditModel class.

Having a look at GetEnumSelectList, you will notice that the Intellisense specifies that it returns an IEnumerable<SelectListItem> in Figure 3-7.

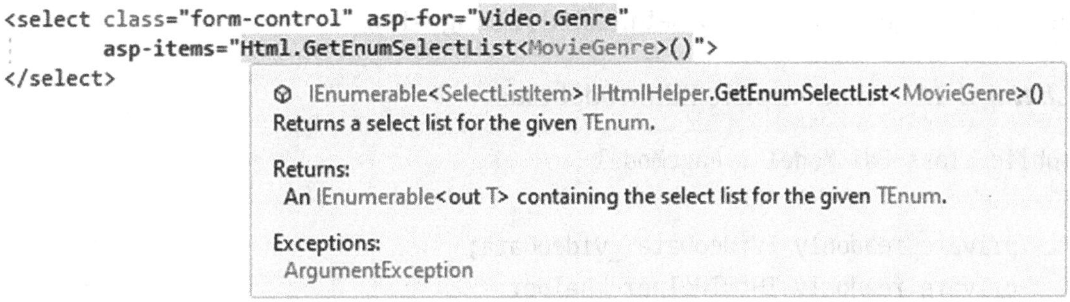

```
<select class="form-control" asp-for="Video.Genre"
        asp-items="Html.GetEnumSelectList<MovieGenre>()">
</select>
```

Figure 3-7. *IEnumerable<SelectListItem> Return Type*

I can, therefore, add a property to my EditModel class of IEnumerable<SelectListItem> that will contain the items for the MovieGenre enum (Listing 3-10).

Listing 3-10. The Genres Property

```
public IEnumerable<SelectListItem> Genres { get; set; }
```

This property can now be used with the asp-items tag helper to display the MovieGenre items in my drop-down.

Please note that you will need to bring in the using statements for Microsoft. AspNetCore.Mvc.Rendering and System.Collections.Generic.

Because we are working in the EditModel class, we can't directly reference the HTML helper GetEnumSelectList. That HTML helper is only available on the Razor page. What we can do is tell ASP.NET Core to inject the IHtmlHelper service to the constructor that will allow me to use that helper (Listing 3-11).

Listing 3-11. Injecting the IHtmlHelper Service

```
public EditModel(IVideoData videoData, IHtmlHelper helper)
{
    _videoData = videoData;
}
```

Just as before with the IVideoData service, we can save the IHtmlHelper to a private field and reference that in our OnGet method (Listing 3-12).

Listing 3-12. The Complete EditModel Class

```
public class EditModel : PageModel
{
    private readonly IVideoData _videoData;
    private readonly IHtmlHelper _helper;

    public Video Video { get; set; }
    public IEnumerable<SelectListItem> Genres { get; set; }

    public EditModel(IVideoData videoData, IHtmlHelper helper)
    {
        _videoData = videoData;
        _helper = helper;
    }

    public IActionResult OnGet(int videoId)
    {
        Genres = _helper.GetEnumSelectList<MovieGenre>();
        Video = _videoData.GetVideo(videoId);

        return Video == null ? RedirectToPage("./VideoError", new {
        message = "The video does not exist" }) : (IActionResult)Page();
    }
}
```

You will notice that the line of code Genres = _helper.GetEnumSelectList<Movi eGenre>(); in our OnGet method looks almost identical to the markup we added in the asp-items tag helper in the markup on the Razor page.

We can therefore modify the markup in the `<select>` element's `asp-items` tag helper to reference the `Genres` property on our `EditModel` class.

The code will look as in Listing 3-13.

Listing 3-13. The Modified Markup

```
<select class="form-control" asp-for="Video.Genre" asp-items="Model.Genres">
</select>
```

For clarity, I have included the entire `Edit.cshtml` page's markup (Listing 3-14) so that you can see how it has been modified.

Listing 3-14. The Complete Edit Page Markup

```
@page "{videoId:int}"
@model VideoStore.Pages.Videos.EditModel
@{
    ViewData["Title"] = "Edit";
}

<h1>Editing: @Model.Video.Title</h1>

<form method="post">
    <input type="hidden" asp-for="Video.Id" />
    <div class="form-group">
        <label asp-for="Video.Title"></label>
        <input asp-for="Video.Title" class="form-control" />
    </div>

    <div class="form-group">
        <label asp-for="Video.ReleaseDate"></label>
        <input asp-for="Video.ReleaseDate" class="form-control" />
    </div>

    <div class="form-group">
        <label asp-for="Video.Genre"></label>
        <select class="form-control" asp-for="Video.Genre"
                asp-items="Model.Genres">
        </select>
    </div>
```

```
<div class="form-group">
    <label asp-for="Video.Price"></label>
    <input asp-for="Video.Price" class="form-control" />
</div>

<div class="form-group">
    <label asp-for="Video.LentOut"></label>
    <input asp-for="Video.LentOut" class="form-control" />
</div>

<div class="form-group">
    <label asp-for="Video.LentTo"></label>
    <input asp-for="Video.LentTo" class="form-control" />
</div>

    <button type="submit" class="btn border-primary">Update Video</button>
</form>
```

If you run the web application again, you should still see the same items listed in the drop-down as illustrated in Figure 3-6.

```
▼<div class="form-group">
    <label for="Video_Genre">Genre</label>
    ▼<select class="form-control" data-val="true" data-val-
    required="The Genre field is required." id="Video_Genre"
    name="Video.Genre">
        <option value="0">None</option>
        <option selected="selected" value="1">Action</option>
        <option value="2">Romance</option>
        <option value="3">Drama</option>
        <option value="4">Horror</option>
    </select>
</div>
```

Figure 3-8. *The Generated Markup for the Drop-down*

Looking at the generated markup for the drop-down (Figure 3-8), you will notice that the markup looks a lot like the code in Listing 3-9, where we could manually specify the drop-down items.

This is what tag helpers and HTML helpers allow us to do. They allow us to insert short snippets of HTML markup into our page.

Changing the Data Service

We need to add the logic to save the modified video data to the data store. At the moment, we are only binding the video data to the fields on the form, but we aren't doing anything with the form to be able to save the modifications.

We only have an OnGet method in our EditModel class. Looking at the <form> element on the Razor page, you will see that the method specified is a POST. So working from the bottom up (if you consider the data source at the bottom and the UI at the top as I do), let's modify the IVideoData Interface for the data source first.

We need to add two new portions of logic to our Interface to allow us to work with modified data. These are

- Updating a video

- Saving the changes to the database

I am splitting the logic for the Update and Commit because I want to separate my data service logic.

In other words, I only want my update method to take an existing record and update the properties with the changed data coming in from the Edit form. I also might want to do some additional validation and inspect the changed video data before committing it to the database.

For this reason, I have a separate Save method. Consider the changes to the IVideoData Interface in Listing 3-15.

Listing 3-15. The Modified IVideoData Interface

```
public interface IVideoData
{
    IEnumerable<Video> ListVideos(string title);
    Video GetVideo(int id);
    Video UpdateVideo(Video videoData);
    int Save();
}
```

We will now need to provide implementations for these new methods that we added to the Interface. In other words, we need to modify every class that implements this Interface to provide the implementations for the new methods. At the moment, the only class implementing the IVideoData Interface is our TestData service.

Listing 3-16. The UpdateVideo method

```
public Video UpdateVideo(Video updatedVideoData)
{
    var dbObj = _videoList.SingleOrDefault(x => x.Id == updatedVideoData.Id);
    if (dbObj != null)
    {
        dbObj.Title = updatedVideoData.Title;
        dbObj.ReleaseDate = updatedVideoData.ReleaseDate;
        dbObj.Genre = updatedVideoData.Genre;
        dbObj.Price = updatedVideoData.Price;
        dbObj.LentOut = updatedVideoData.LentOut;
        dbObj.LentTo = updatedVideoData.LentTo;
    }

    return dbObj;
}
```

Add a method to the TestData class called UpdateVideo as illustrated in Listing 3-16. This method is only concerned with updating the video data. It takes the ID from the updatedVideoData object and tries to find a match in the _videoList test data.

If a match is found, then the object found is updated with the values in the updatedVideoData.

We also need to provide an implementation for the Save method, as we are currently not saving any data. Remember, we are only working with test data here. We are doing this so that we can get all the moving parts in place before hooking our web application up to real data.

Listing 3-17. The Save Method

```
public int Save() => 0;
```

This means that we can simply return 0 for the Save method (Listing 3-17) because we are not actually going to save any data in our TestData service.

Validate Edited Data and Display Validation Errors

There is a saying that states, never trust a skinny cook. Well, the same is true in software development when it comes to users. Never trust the data entered on a form by a user. Doing so will get you into trouble in no time.

Many years ago, I was working on a project where the validation was incorrectly implemented on a form. It was a technical database that contained recipes for beauty products. These recipes were then loaded into the manufacturing process that integrated with that company's ERP system. The ERP system then created jobs for the manufacturing process to run.

Now and then, some of these recipes were changed to accommodate new raw materials, new measurements, and so on to affect the net quantity or volume of the finished product.

Yes, companies do sometimes alter the weight or volume of products. Just look at how small chocolates have become. Where I live, I used to be able to buy my favorite 100g chocolate, but now, sadly, we only get 90g chocolates.

The form that was used to enter and modify recipes provided adequate validation for the inputs from the user. It then displayed the updated entries in a data grid before saving that to the database. The data grid was the last check for the user to verify that the data was entered correctly before submitting it.

A few weeks after the application was installed and signed off, the client informed us that saving or updating recipes no longer worked. The application was presenting the user with an error. The screenshot they sent showed that this was an unhandled exception.

It turned out that while the users could only enter the validated information via the form fields, they found out that they could modify that data in the data grid before submitting it.

The data grid was only meant as a way of verifying the entered data and needed to be read-only, which it wasn't. When they figured out that they could modify the data directly inside the grid, all the previous validation performed on the entry form was irrelevant.

It's like that movie with the dinosaurs where Jeff Goldblum states that life finds a way. Well, when dealing with end users, they will find a way of entering invalid data.

With this chestnut in mind, and armed with what we know about end users, we need to provide validation for the entered data on the form. Start by adding an OnPost method (Listing 3-18) to your EditModel class.

Listing 3-18. The OnPost Method

```
public IActionResult OnPost()
{
    return Page();
}
```

It might be tempting to add a whole lot of if statements here to perform validation of the entered data. Fortunately for us, ASP.NET Core provides an easy way to perform input validation. We can add data annotations to our Video model inside the VideoStore.Core project.

Be sure to add the required namespace via the System.ComponentModel. DataAnnotations using statement.

Make a slight change to your Video model by adding the [Required] annotation to the Title property as illustrated in Listing 3-19.

Listing 3-19. Adding a Required Field Validation to Title

```
using System;
using System.ComponentModel.DataAnnotations;

namespace VideoStore.Core
{
    public class Video
    {
        public int Id { get; set; }
        [Required]
        public string Title { get; set; }
        public DateTime ReleaseDate { get; set; }
        public MovieGenre Genre { get; set; }
        public double Price { get; set; }
```

```
    public bool LentOut { get; set; }
    public string LentTo { get; set; }
  }
}
```

We can now use the `asp-validation-for` tag helper to provide some feedback to the user on the form if an entered value is incorrect. In your `Edit.cshtml` Razor page, modify the div containing the `Video.Title` input as illustrated in Listing 3-20.

Listing 3-20. Validation Added to Video.Title

```
<div class="form-group">
    <label asp-for="Video.Title"></label>
    <input asp-for="Video.Title" class="form-control" />
    <span class="text-danger" asp-validation-for="Video.Title"></span>
</div>
```

Switch back over to the `EditModel` class, and because the video ID on the form is the one that we want to modify, we can add the `[BindProperty]` attribute to the `Video` property.

You will remember from the previous chapter that this will change the property to be an input and an output property.

The modified property will need to be changed to look as illustrated in Listing 3-21.

Listing 3-21. Modifying the Video Property

```
[BindProperty]
public Video Video { get; set; }
```

Therefore, when the user clicks the Update Video button, the `Video` property will be populated with the values entered on the form.

With all this in place, and with the data annotations on my `Video` model, validating the entered data is very easy. Whenever ASP.NET Core performs model binding on my `Video` model, the framework keeps a record of everything that happens to that data inside something we call `ModelState`. I can now check to see if that `ModelState` is valid before updating any of my entered form data.

Go ahead and change the OnPost method to check the ModelState as illustrated in Listing 3-22, and if valid, update the video data.

Listing 3-22. Modified OnPost Method

```
public IActionResult OnPost()
{
    if (ModelState.IsValid)
    {
        _ = _videoData.UpdateVideo(Video);
        _ = _videoData.Save();
        return RedirectToPage("./Detail", new { videoId = Video.Id });
    }
    Genres = _helper.GetEnumSelectList<MovieGenre>();
    return Page();
}
```

You will also notice that I rebind the Genres property because ASP.NET Core is stateless and the values are not persisted during the OnPost method. I also tell the web application that if the ModelState is valid, and the video has been updated, then it must redirect to the Detail page.

You will remember that we added the videoId in the @page directive of the Detail Razor page. This is why I pass the Video.Id in the route values on the RedirectToPage method in the OnPost method of the Edit page.

Running the application and trying to enter a blank title for the video will result in the form validation displaying a validation error on the Edit page as seen in Figure 3-9.

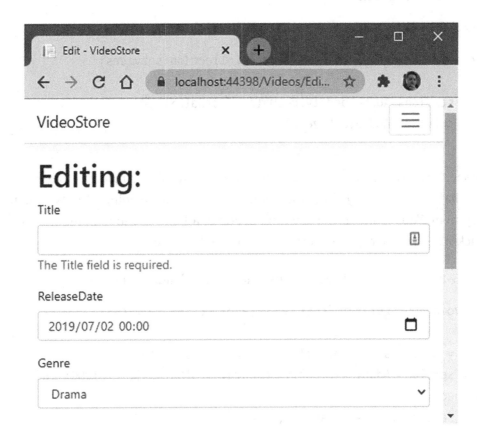

Figure 3-9. *The Form Validation at Work*

This is what we wanted. We do not want the user to update the video without specifying a title for the video. But there is another problem (well, only while we are in development, anyway). Modify the video title, and click the Update Video button.

You will be redirected to the Detail page, but you will notice that the details you changed are not being displayed on the Detail page. This is not a bug, and it is because we did something way back when we specified the IVideoData service in the ConfigureServices method of the Startup.cs file.

You will remember (as illustrated in Listing 3-23) that we specified that whenever someone needs an instance of IVideoData, provide them an instance of our TestData class.

But we told the services collection to provide a scoped instance by calling the services.AddScoped method.

Listing 3-23. The ConfigureServices Method in the Startup.cs

```
public void ConfigureServices(IServiceCollection services)
{
    _ = services.AddScoped<IVideoData, TestData>();
    _ = services.AddRazorPages();
}
```

To see the modified data in our test data, we want to add a singleton instance of our TestData (Listing 3-24). This is something we will only be doing while we are in development. You would most likely want to add in a TODO here to remember to change this back when we are ready to work against a real database.

Listing 3-24. Provide a Singleton Instance of TestData for Testing

```
public void ConfigureServices(IServiceCollection services)
{
    //_ = services.AddScoped<IVideoData, TestData>();
    _ = services.AddSingleton<IVideoData, TestData>(); // TODO: Change to
    scoped
    _ = services.AddRazorPages();
}
```

With this change made, run your web application again and modify the video data and save your changes. You will see that the details displayed on the Detail page have been updated to display your modifications.

AddSingleton vs. AddScoped vs. AddTransient

I want to pause here for a second to discuss the different lifetimes that we can add for the services. You can register the following lifetimes for the services collection:

- Singleton
- Scoped
- Transient

Each one of these is leveraged during dependency injection, and you will need to make sure that you choose the appropriate lifetime for each registered service.

Singleton

When creating a singleton lifetime service (using the `AddSingleton` method), every subsequent request will make use of the same instance. This means that in applications that process requests (like our web application), the singleton services are disposed of when the application is shut down (because the `ServiceProvider` is disposed).

Scoped

A scoped lifetime is only created once per client request (or connection). As you saw in the code in Listing 3-23, we register scoped services using the `AddScoped` method. This means that with applications that process requests, scoped services will be disposed of at the end of the request.

Transient

A service created with a transient lifetime will be created each time they are requested from the service container. In other words, you are telling ASP.NET Core that every time the service is requested, you want a new instance of that service. Transient services are therefore disposed of at the end of the request.

Implementing IValidatableObject

If you need to perform slightly more complex validations, you can do so by implementing the `IValidatableObject` on your model. Think of the Lent Out check box on the form. If this is checked, we want to make the Lent To field required. How can we do this? Well, this is where the `IValidatableObject` Interface comes in handy.

Open the `Video` class in the `VideoStore.Core` project, and implement this Interface. In the `Validate` method, provide your custom implementation for the `LentTo` property as illustrated in the code in Listing 3-25.

Listing 3-25. Implementing the IValidatableObject

```
using System;
using System.Collections.Generic;
using System.ComponentModel.DataAnnotations;
```

```csharp
namespace VideoStore.Core
{
    public class Video : IValidatableObject
    {
        public int Id { get; set; }
        [Required]
        public string Title { get; set; }
        public DateTime ReleaseDate { get; set; }
        public MovieGenre Genre { get; set; }
        public double Price { get; set; }
        public bool LentOut { get; set; }
        public string LentTo { get; set; }

        public IEnumerable<ValidationResult> Validate(ValidationContext
        validationContext)
        {
            var property = new[] { nameof(LentTo) };
            var validationResults = new List<ValidationResult>();

            if (LentOut && string.IsNullOrEmpty(LentTo))
            {
                validationResults.Add(new ValidationResult("Please enter a
                name for Lent To", property));
            }

            return validationResults;
        }
    }
}
```

Implementing the Validate method of the Interface allows us to provide some custom validation functionality. In our case, we want to make the Lent To field required if it is empty and the user has checked the Lent Out check box.

We also need to add the asp-validation-for tag helper to the Video.LentTo input on the Edit.cshtml Razor page (Listing 3-26).

Listing 3-26. Add the Validation Tag Helper to LentTo

```
<div class="form-group">
    <label asp-for="Video.LentTo"></label>
    <input asp-for="Video.LentTo" class="form-control" />
    <span class="text-danger" asp-validation-for="Video.LentTo"></span>
</div>
```

If you try to update a video by specifying that you have lent out the video, but do not provide a name of the person you lent it to, the form validation will display the required validation message as seen in Figure 3-10.

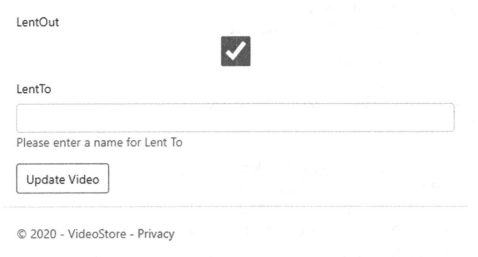

© 2020 - VideoStore - Privacy

Figure 3-10. *Validating LentTo Field*

The custom validation can become much more complex than the simple custom validation I illustrated. What is important to note, however, is that when the validation provided out of the box doesn't meet your needs, you can provide the custom validation you require using the IValidatableObject Interface.

I have not provided any validation in this book for the other properties on the Video model. I will leave these for you to play around with. What I do want to do, however, is highlight the Edit form's labels.

Looking back to Figures 3-9 and 3-10, you will notice that the labels are rendered on the web page in the same way the property names are spelled. In other words, the video's release date is displayed as ReleaseDate and the Lent Out check box as LentOut and so on. We can control this behavior once again, by modifying the Video model.

You might need to bring in the System.ComponentModel namespace via a using statement.

In Listing 3-27, you will see the complete Video model code. Above each property that you want to change the display name of, add the [DisplayName] annotation.

Listing 3-27. Complete Video Model Code

```
using System;
using System.Collections.Generic;
using System.ComponentModel;
using System.ComponentModel.DataAnnotations;

namespace VideoStore.Core
{
    public class Video : IValidatableObject
    {
        public int Id { get; set; }
        [Required, DisplayName("Video Title")]
        public string Title { get; set; }
        [DisplayName("Release Date")]
        public DateTime ReleaseDate { get; set; }
        public MovieGenre Genre { get; set; }
        public double Price { get; set; }
        [DisplayName("Lent Out")]
        public bool LentOut { get; set; }
        [DisplayName("On Loan to")]
        public string LentTo { get; set; }

        public IEnumerable<ValidationResult> Validate(ValidationContext
        validationContext)
        {
            var property = new[] { nameof(LentTo) };
            var validationResults = new List<ValidationResult>();
```

```
        if (LentOut && string.IsNullOrEmpty(LentTo))
        {
            validationResults.Add(new ValidationResult("Please enter a
            name for Lent To", property));
        }

        return validationResults;
    }
  }
}
```

You can now control exactly how the various properties are displayed on the form. You can even combine several annotations as seen on the Title property where we added [Required, DisplayName("Video Title")] in a single line.

Run your web application to see the new display names for your properties on your Edit form.

Adding a New Video

Our video store web application would be as useful as a one-legged chicken in a chicken race without the ability to add additional videos. We have added all the logic to edit an existing video, but we can't, as yet, add a new video.

Some folks prefer to create a separate Add page for this purpose, but what you will find is that much of the logic will be the same as the Edit page's logic. We can repurpose the Edit page to act as both an Edit page and an Add page.

To add a new video, I want to add a button to the list of videos, next to the search bar. This way, if the video that the user searched for doesn't exist, they can easily just add the video. Modify the <form> to include the add button as illustrated in Listing 3-28.

Listing 3-28. The Modified List Page

```
<form method="get">
    <div class="form-group">
        <div class="input-group">
            <input type="search"
                   class="form-control"
                   asp-for="SearchQuery" />
```

```
            <button class="btn btn-group">
                <i class="fas fa-search"></i>
            </button>
            <a asp-page="./Edit" class="btn btn-group">
                <i class="fas fa-plus"></i>
            </a>
        </div>
    </div>
</form>
```

There is, however, a small catch. When we created the Edit page, we told it that we will pass through a video ID in the URL. We did this in the @page directive on the Edit. cshtml page. Therefore, it will only respond to a route that contains a video ID.

To fix this issue, we need to tell the @page directive that the video ID in the route is an optional value. We, therefore, need to specify the @page directive as @page "{videoId:int?}" with a question mark after the int to denote that the video ID is nullable. To put this into context, the Edit.cshtml page needs to look as in Listing 3-29.

Listing 3-29. The Edit.cshtml Page's @page Directive

```
@page "{videoId:int?}"
@model VideoStore.Pages.Videos.EditModel
@{
    ViewData["Title"] = "Edit";
}

<h1>Editing: @Model.Video.Title</h1>
```

With this bit in place, we also need to modify the OnGet method of our EditModel class. The code in Listing 3-30 contains the modified OnGet method.

Listing 3-30. The Modified OnGet Method

```
public IActionResult OnGet(int? videoId)
{
    Genres = _helper.GetEnumSelectList<MovieGenre>();
    Video = videoId.HasValue
        ? _videoData.GetVideo(videoId.Value)
```

```
    : new Video
    {
        ReleaseDate = DateTime.Now.Date
    };

    return Video == null ? RedirectToPage("./VideoError", new { message =
    "The video does not exist" }) : (IActionResult)Page();
}
```

Here, we are telling the code that the videoId is a nullable parameter. If that videoId has a value, then go out to our data service and fetch a video with the specified ID.

If the videoId is null, then instantiate a new instance of the Video and default the ReleaseDate to the current date. While this takes care of the instance where a user adds a new video, we need to modify our data service to allow for that addition to be added to the list of videos (and later on, the database). Let's do that next.

Modifying the Data Access Service

Working again from the IVideoData Interface, we need to add a method to add a video called AddVideo (or whatever you choose) as seen in Listing 3-31.

Listing 3-31. Modified IVideoData Interface to Allow Add

```
using System.Collections.Generic;
using VideoStore.Core;

namespace VideoStore.Data
{
    public interface IVideoData
    {
        IEnumerable<Video> ListVideos(string title);
        Video GetVideo(int id);
        Video UpdateVideo(Video videoData);
        Video AddVideo(Video newVideo);
        int Save();
    }
}
```

Because we have modified our Interface, we need to provide the implementation in all classes implementing our Interface which is, in our case, just the TestData class. Add the method illustrated in Listing 3-32 to the TestData class.

Listing 3-32. The AddVideo Method in the TestData Class

```
public Video AddVideo(Video newVideo)
{
    newVideo.Id = _videoList.Max(x => x.Id) + 1;
    _videoList.Add(newVideo);
    return newVideo;
}
```

When we eventually start working with a real database, the new video ID will be auto-incremented in the database table. For now, while we are working with the TestData class, our video IDs are hardcoded in the list of videos. We, therefore, need to add the line of code newVideo.Id = _videoList.Max(x => x.Id) + 1 to simulate the incrementing of the video ID in the database. This is a bit of silly, messy code. Its only purpose is to allow us to be able to test our web application and to simulate the workings of a real data service.

Once we create our real data service, it too will implement the IVideoData Interface along with all the required methods. These implementations will look very different from those in our TestData class.

All that remains for us to do now is to modify the OnPost method of the EditModel class.

Modifying the OnPost Method

The last bit we need to do is really simple. If we have a Video.Id that is greater than 0, then we are updating an existing video. If the Video.Id is 0, then we are adding a new video.

Listing 3-33. The Modified OnPost Method

```
public IActionResult OnPost()
{
    if (ModelState.IsValid)
```

```
    {
        _ = Video.Id > 0 ? _videoData.UpdateVideo(Video) : _videoData.
        AddVideo(Video);
        _ = _videoData.Save();
        return RedirectToPage("./Detail", new { videoId = Video.Id });
    }
    Genres = _helper.GetEnumSelectList<MovieGenre>();
    return Page();
}
```

The modified OnPost method can be seen in Listing 3-33. Run the web application, and add a new video. The new video will be added to our Video List, allowing you to edit it and save the changes.

Working with TempData

Having repurposed the Edit page to act as an Add page too means that we might need to change some labels and headings. You might want to remove the text "Editing:" from the <h1> tag in the Edit.cshtml page.

You might also want to change the text of the Update Video button as well. I will leave this as homework for you to do, but what I do want to discuss is the notion of TempData. If I update or add a video, I want the Detail page to respond accordingly with a suitable message. Think of a message dialog that is displayed in a traditional Windows Forms application. I want to notify the user that an update or an addition has taken place.

In ASP.NET Core, you can access the TempData for Razor pages (this resides in the Microsoft.AspNetCore.Mvc.RazorPages namespace) or for Controllers (residing in the Microsoft.AspNetCore.Mvc namespace).

TempData will store information until that information is read in another request. This means that once it's read, it's dead. You can use the Keep and Peek methods to have a look at the information without deleting it at the end of the request. The Keep method does what the name suggests, which is to mark the information in TempData as data that should be retained. This is, however, not something we will be doing.

As illustrated in Listing 3-34, you will see that I want to decide which message to pass in my TempData. Before the _videoData.Save() method is called, I perform the same conditional decision as to when I was deciding whether I should update or add a video.

That is, if the video has an ID greater than 0, then I must be updating a video. If not, then I'm adding.

Listing 3-34. Pass Conditional TempData Message

```
public IActionResult OnPost()
{
    if (ModelState.IsValid)
    {
        TempData["CommitMessage"] = Video.Id > 0 ? "Video Updated" : "Video
        Added";
        _ = Video.Id > 0 ? _videoData.UpdateVideo(Video) : _videoData.
        AddVideo(Video);
        _ = _videoData.Save();
        return RedirectToPage("./Detail", new { videoId = Video.Id });
    }
    Genres = _helper.GetEnumSelectList<MovieGenre>();
    return Page();
}
```

I can now go to my `DetailModel` class and create a property called `CommitMessage` that has the [`TempData`] attribute. You can see this code in Listing 3-35.

Listing 3-35. The DetailModel Page

```
public class DetailModel : PageModel
{
    private readonly IVideoData _videoData;

    public Video Video { get; set; }

    [TempData]
    public string CommitMessage { get; set; }

    public DetailModel(IVideoData videoData)
    {
        _videoData = videoData;
    }
```

```
public IActionResult OnGet(int videoId)
{
    Video = _videoData.GetVideo(videoId);

    return Video == null ? RedirectToPage("./VideoError", new { message
    = "The video does not exist" }) : (IActionResult)Page();
}
}
```

Now that I have a property decorated with the TempData attribute, ASP.NET Core will read the TempData for the Razor page and see if it contains a key called CommitMessage. It is important that the property name and the key in the TempData match; otherwise, ASP. NET Core can't assign the value stored inside TempData to the property.

So with that change done, all that remains is to check the existence of a value in TempData and display the message on the Detail.cshtml Razor page. The code illustrated in Listing 3-36 shows the commit message added just underneath the <h1> video title.

Listing 3-36. The Detail Razor Page Commit Message

```
@page "{videoId:int}"
@model VideoStore.Pages.Videos.DetailModel
@{
    ViewData["Title"] = "Detail";
}

<h1>@Model.Video.Title</h1>

@if (Model.CommitMessage != null)
{
    <div class="alert alert-info">@Model.CommitMessage</div>
}

<div>
    Catalog ID: @Model.Video.Id
</div>
<div>
    Release Date: @Model.Video.ReleaseDate.ToString("dd MMMM yyyy")
</div>
```

```
<div>
    Genre: @Model.Video.Genre
</div>
<div>
    Price: $@Model.Video.Price
</div>
<div>
    Lent Out: @Html.CheckBoxFor(x => x.Video.LentOut)
</div>

@if (Model.Video.LentOut == true)
{
    <div>
        Lent To: @Model.Video.LentTo
    </div>
}

<a asp-page="./List" class="btn btn-outline-primary">Back to Videos</a>
```

Now, when you add or update a video, the appropriate message will be displayed on the Detail Razor page. If you refresh the page, the message will disappear. This is what we wanted. It is only temporary data.

If you modify the markup that displays the commit message and specify that the temporary data must be kept, then the result is quite different.

Modify the section of markup in the Detail.cshtml Razor page to tell ASP.NET to keep the TempData with the key of CommitMessage. The code is illustrated in Listing 3-37.

Listing 3-37. Keeping TempData

```
@if (Model.CommitMessage != null)
{
    TempData.Keep("CommitMessage");
    <div class="alert alert-info">@Model.CommitMessage</div>
}
```

This time, when you see the commit message on the Detail.cshtml Razor page, and hit the refresh button, the message remains there.

Changing the TempData Provider

By default, the provider for TempData is cookie based. You can see this in the browser's DevTools (I am using Google Chrome - Figure 3-11). With the line of code `TempData.Keep` illustrated in Listing 3-37 in place, add a new video and open up DevTools when you see the `Detail` page.

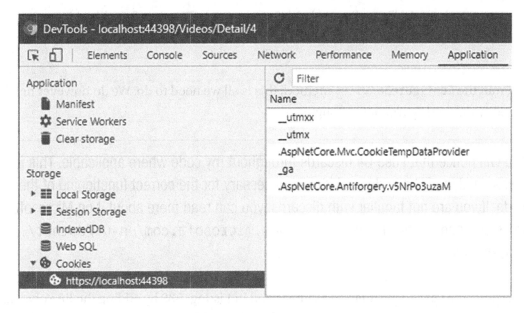

Figure 3-11. *The Default Cookie-Based TempData Provider*

Head on over to the Application tab, and expand the Cookies node under Storage. There, you will see `AspNetCore.Mvc.CookieTempDataProvider` listed. You can change this behavior by enabling the session-based `TempData` provider instead. We need to do this in the `Startup` class for the application.

As illustrated in Listing 3-38, you need to add the extension method `AddSessionStateTempDataProvider` to the `AddRazorPages()` method. You must also add the line of code `_ = services.AddSession()`.

Listing 3-38. The ConfigureServices Method

```
public void ConfigureServices(IServiceCollection services)
{
    //_ = services.AddScoped<IVideoData, TestData>();
    _ = services.AddSingleton<IVideoData, TestData>(); // TODO: Change to
    scoped
    _ = services.AddRazorPages().AddSessionStateTempDataProvider();
    _ = services.AddSession();
}
```

From the ConfigureServices method, this is all we need to do. We do however need to modify the Configure method slightly.

You will notice that I use C# discards throughout my code where applicable. This is just something I like to do, and it's not necessary for the correct functioning of the code. If you are not familiar with discards, you can read more about it on Microsoft Docs at the following link: https://docs.microsoft.com/en-us/dotnet/csharp/discards.

Modify the Configure method as illustrated in Listing 3-39 by adding the line of code _ = app.UseSession() before the call to the UseEndpoints extension method.

Listing 3-39. The Modified Configure Method

```
public void Configure(IApplicationBuilder app, IWebHostEnvironment env)
{
    if (env.IsDevelopment())
    {
        _ = app.UseDeveloperExceptionPage();
    }
    else
    {
        _ = app.UseExceptionHandler("/Error");
        _ = app.UseHsts();
    }
```

```
_ = app.UseHttpsRedirection();
_ = app.UseStaticFiles();

_ = app.UseRouting();

_ = app.UseAuthorization();

_ = app.UseSession();

_ = app.UseEndpoints(endpoints =>
    {
        _ = endpoints.MapRazorPages();
    });
}
```

Once again, run the web application, add a new video, and open up DevTools when you see the Detail page.

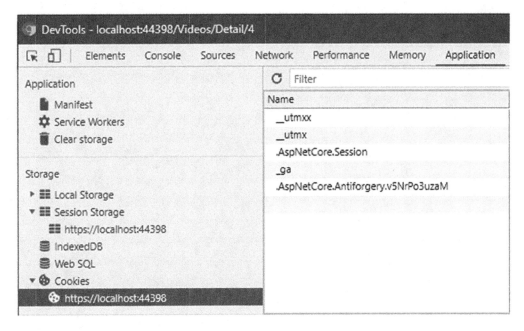

Figure 3-12. *The Session-Based TempData Provider*

This time, on the Application tab under the Cookies node under Storage, you will see that AspNetCore.Session is the provider in use (Figure 3-12).

CHAPTER 4

EF Core and SQL Server

The ultimate goal of our web application is to work against a real SQL database. Up until now, we have only been working with our `TestData` service. You will remember that we created this service to mimic the workings of a real SQL database, just while we were busy developing the foundation of our application.

Now, however, it is time to take a look at installing Entity Framework Core and start working with real data. Before I go into that, let's pause for a minute and have a look at what Entity Framework Core is exactly.

Entity Framework Core

If you have worked with Entity Framework before, this will feel very familiar to you. Entity Framework Core (or EF Core for short) is the lightweight version of Entity Framework. It is extensible, open source, and because it is termed "Core," you know that it works cross-platform. EF Core also serves as an O/RM. This allows EF Core to

- Enable developers to work against a database using .NET objects

- Remove the need to write data access code

If you are used to rolling your own when it comes to data access code, then EF Core might be a bit of a paradigm shift for you. It does make life a lot easier though, however, some developers hate having to use it. Nevertheless, EF Core is here to stay, and seeing as it supports many database engines, I doubt that it will be going away anytime soon.

See the list of EF Core database providers at the following link: `https://docs. microsoft.com/en-us/ef/core/providers/?tabs=dotnet-core-cli`.

© Dirk Strauss 2021
D. Strauss, *Creating ASP.NET Core Web Applications*, https://doi.org/10.1007/978-1-4842-6828-5_4

The convenience of not having to write a lot of the data access code, having it generated for you by EF Core, is beneficial. When you use EF Core, the data access is done using a model. This comprises entity classes and a context object. This represents a database session.

We will come back to the context object later on, but know that this object allows you to query and save data. Entity Framework supports the following model development approaches:

- You can generate a model from an existing database.

- You can manually create a model to match your database.

- Created models can be used to create databases using EF Migrations. EF Migrations also allow you to update the database when your model changes.

This is in a nutshell what EF Core is all about. Let's have a look at installing EF Core next.

Install Entity Framework

When we first created our web application, we created the VideoStore.Data project. The idea was to separate concerns in our solution. This project is where we will be installing EF Core.

Right-click the VideoStore.Data project, and click the Manage NuGet Packages link (you can also right-click the Dependencies node).

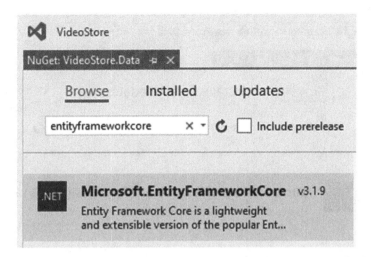

Figure 4-1. *Browsing for the Entity Framework Core NuGet Package*

From the Browse tab, search for the Microsoft.EntityFrameworkCore package (Figure 4-1). The latest version for me is 3.1.9, but for you, it might be different. Secondly, we need to install a database provider. We will be using SQL Server, so search for and install the Microsoft.EntityFrameworkCore.SqlServer NuGet package (Figure 4-2).

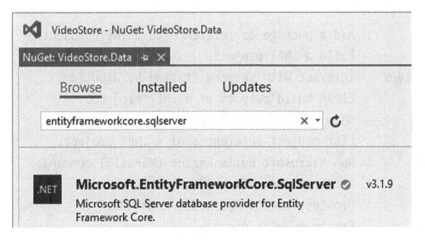

Figure 4-2. *EF Core Database Provider*

The last NuGet package we will be installing is the Microsoft.EntityFrameworkCore. Design NuGet package (Figure 4-3).

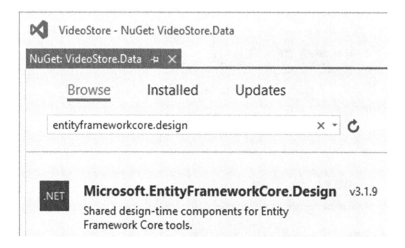

Figure 4-3. *EF Core Design-Time Components*

It is important to note that you could also have installed the required packages from the command line using the dotnet add command. Open the Command Prompt, and type in dotnet -h to see the output in Listing 4-1.

Listing 4-1. The dotnet Commands

```
SDK commands:
  add           Add a package or reference to a .NET project.
  build         Build a .NET project.
  build-server  Interact with servers started by a build.
  clean         Clean build outputs of a .NET project.
  help          Show command line help.
  list          List project references of a .NET project.
  msbuild       Run Microsoft Build Engine (MSBuild) commands.
  new           Create a new .NET project or file.
  nuget         Provides additional NuGet commands.
  pack          Create a NuGet package.
  publish       Publish a .NET project for deployment.
  remove        Remove a package or reference from a .NET project.
  restore       Restore dependencies specified in a .NET project.
  run           Build and run a .NET project output.
  sln           Modify Visual Studio solution files.
```

store	Store specified assemblies in the runtime package store.
test	Run unit tests using test runner specified in a .NET project.
tool	Install or manage tools that extend the .NET experience.
vstest	Run Microsoft Test Engine (VSTest) commands.

Additional commands from bundled tools:

dev-certs	Create and manage development certificates.
fsi	Start F# Interactive / execute F# scripts.
sql-cache	SQL Server cache command-line tools.
user-secrets	Manage development user secrets.
watch	Start a file watcher that runs a command when files change.

Have a look at the following link to see more about the dotnet add command: https://docs.microsoft.com/en-us/dotnet/core/tools/dotnet-add-package. Lastly, if you open the .csproj file of VideoStore.Data, you will see the package references we just added (Listing 4-2).

Listing 4-2. VideoStore.Data csproj File

```
<Project Sdk="Microsoft.NET.Sdk">

  <PropertyGroup>
    <TargetFramework>netcoreapp3.1</TargetFramework>
  </PropertyGroup>

  <ItemGroup>
    <PackageReference Include="Microsoft.EntityFrameworkCore"
    Version="3.1.9" />
    <PackageReference Include="Microsoft.EntityFrameworkCore.Design"
    Version="3.1.9">
      <PrivateAssets>all</PrivateAssets>
      <IncludeAssets>runtime; build; native; contentfiles; analyzers;
      buildtransitive</IncludeAssets>
    </PackageReference>
```

```
  <PackageReference Include="Microsoft.EntityFrameworkCore.SqlServer"
  Version="3.1.9" />
</ItemGroup>

<ItemGroup>
  <ProjectReference Include="..\VideoStore.Core\VideoStore.Core.csproj" />
</ItemGroup>

</Project>
```

The addition of EF Core to the VideoStore.Data project is all we need to do right now. The next task on our list is to look at DbContext.

Implement DbContext

An instance of a DbContext will represent a session with the database. This will allow us to save and query entity instances. What we will be doing is to create a class and derive it from DbContext.

This class will contain properties of type DbSet<T> that represent each entity in the model. Right-click the VideoStore.Data project, and add a new class called VideoDbContext to the project.

Be sure to add the Microsoft.EntityFrameworkCore and VideoStore.Core namespaces to your class.

With your VideoDbContext class created, inherit the class from DbContext as illustrated in Listing 4-3.

Listing 4-3. The VideoDbContext Class

```
namespace VideoStore.Data
{
    public class VideoDbContext : DbContext
    {
    }
}
```

Our application works with videos, so I know that I will need to add a property to the `VideoDbContext` class of type `DbSet<Video>`. The `DbSet` tells the Entity Framework that I want to query, add, delete, and update videos.

While Entity Framework might understand what DbSet is telling it, it might not immediately be obvious to a developer. I agree that the name DbSet does not make the purpose of this class obvious. Whenever I am faced with trying to figure out what a particular class or method does, I take a look at the metadata. To do this, click the DbSet as seen in Listing 4-4 and press F12. You can now see exactly what this class does. The code comments will definitely help you understand more.

Modify the `VideoDbContext` class as illustrated in Listing 4-4.

Listing 4-4. The Videos Property Added to VideoDbContext

```
using Microsoft.EntityFrameworkCore;
using VideoStore.Core;

namespace VideoStore.Data
{
    public class VideoDbContext : DbContext
    {
        public DbSet<Video> Videos { get; set; }
    }
}
```

We can now use this property on the `VideoDbContext` to work with our database.

Specify Database Connection Strings

The next thing we need to do is add some code that will tell the Entity Framework what database we want to use. We will be using LocalDB. It is installed when you install Visual Studio (I am using Visual Studio 2019) and is perfect for what we want to do right now.

To check if LocalDB is installed, run the command in the Command Prompt as seen in Listing 4-5.

Listing 4-5. Check If LocalDb Is Installed

```
Sqllocaldb info
```

You should see the instances of LocalDB listed in the Command Prompt as illustrated in Figure 4-4.

We only have a single instance of LocalDB which is MSSQLLocalDB, but if you work with Umbraco, for example, you might have additional LocalDB instances.

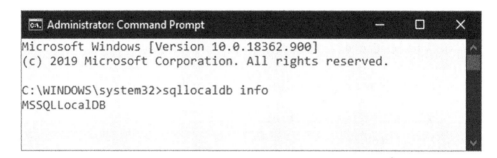

Figure 4-4. *The LocalDB Instances Listed*

In our application, however, we will be using the built-in LocalDB database, and that is what is listed in the output displayed in Figure 4-4. To get more information about the MSSQLLocalDB instance, run the command as illustrated in Listing 4-6.

Listing 4-6. Getting Additional Info for MSSQLLocalDB

```
Sqllocaldb info MSSQLLocalDB
```

This will list some more details about the LocalDB instance (in this case MSSQLLocalDB) currently on your machine (Figure 4-5).

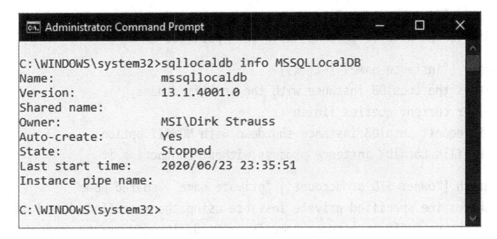

Figure 4-5. *Viewing More Information on MSSQLLocalDB*

As you could have guessed, adding -? after sqllocaldb command in the Command
Prompt will list the available commands you can run. These are seen in Listing 4-7.

Listing 4-7. The Available LocalDB Commands

```
C:\WINDOWS\system32>sqllocaldb -?
Microsoft (R) SQL Server Express LocalDB Command Line Tool
Version 13.0.1601.5
Copyright (c) Microsoft Corporation.  All rights reserved.

Usage: SqlLocalDB operation [parameters...]

Operations:

  -?
    Prints this information

create|c ["instance name" [version-number] [-s]]
    Creates a new LocalDB instance with a specified name and version
    If the [version-number] parameter is omitted, it defaults to the
    latest LocalDB version installed in the system.
    -s starts the new LocalDB instance after it's created

delete|d ["instance name"]
    Deletes the LocalDB instance with the specified name
```

start|s ["instance name"]
  Starts the LocalDB instance with the specified name

stop|p ["instance name" [-i|-k]]
  Stops the LocalDB instance with the specified name,
  after current queries finish
  -i request LocalDB instance shutdown with NOWAIT option
  -k kills LocalDB instance process without contacting it

share|h ["owner SID or account"] "private name" "shared name"
  Shares the specified private instance using the specified shared name.
  If the user SID or account name is omitted, it defaults to current
  user.

unshare|u ["shared name"]
  Stops the sharing of the specified shared LocalDB instance.

info|i
  Lists all existing LocalDB instances owned by the current user
  and all shared LocalDB instances.

info|i "instance name"
  Prints the information about the specified LocalDB instance.

versions|v
  Lists all LocalDB versions installed on the computer.

trace|t on|off
  Turns tracing on and off

SqlLocalDB treats spaces as delimiters. It is necessary to surround
instance names that contain spaces and special characters with quotes.
For example:
  SqlLocalDB create "My LocalDB Instance"

The instance name can sometimes be omitted, as indicated above, or
specified as "". In this case, the reference is to the default LocalDB
instance "MSSQLLocalDB".

You can also see the LocalDB instance in Visual Studio by going to the View menu and clicking the SQL Server Object Explorer menu. You can also press Ctrl+\, Ctrl+S to open SQL Server Object Explorer. This instance may contain one or more databases.

It is this LocalDB instance that we will use during development, but we need to create a connection to it inside our Video Store application. The place to do it is in the appsettings.json file. You will remember that we added the page title for the Video List page here. This time, all we are going to do is to add a new section called ConnectionStrings as seen in Listing 4-8.

Listing 4-8. Connection Strings Added to appsettings.json

```
{
  "Logging": {
    "LogLevel": {
      "Default": "Information",
      "Microsoft": "Warning",
      "Microsoft.Hosting.Lifetime": "Information"
    }
  },
  "AllowedHosts": "*",
  "VideoListPageTitle": "Video Store - Videos List",
  "ConnectionStrings": {
    "VideoConn": "Data Source=(localdb)\\MSSQLLocalDB;Initial
Catalog=VideoStore;Integrated Security=True;"
  }
}
```

The ConnectionStrings section is purposefully plural because this alludes to the fact that you can add multiple connection strings to this configuration section. Inside the ConnectionStrings section, we define key and value pairs for the various database connections that we want to use.

For our database connection, we have simply added a key called VideoConn and a value that defines the connection to our LocalDB database.

One thing to note, however, is that the Initial Catalog (which specifies our database) specifies a database called VideoStore. This database doesn't exist yet, but that's okay for now. We now need a way to tell the DbContext about the connection to the database we want to use. We do this in the ConfigureServices method in the Startup.cs class.

You must add the Microsoft.EntityFrameworkCore namespace to the Startup class.

Change the ConfigureServices method in the Startup class as illustrated in Listing 4-9.

Listing 4-9. The ConfigureServices Method

```
public void ConfigureServices(IServiceCollection services)
{
    services.AddDbContextPool<VideoDbContext>(dbContextOptns =>
    {
        dbContextOptns.UseSqlServer(
            Configuration.GetConnectionString("VideoConn"));
    });

    _ = services.AddSingleton<IVideoData, TestData>(); // TODO: Change to
                                                                scoped
    _ = services.AddRazorPages().AddSessionStateTempDataProvider();
    _ = services.AddSession();
}
```

By bringing in the Entity Framework Core namespace, we can use the UseSqlServer method to tell the Entity Framework about the DbContext that I'm using in my application. We are also telling it to use DbContext pooling. This allows for increased throughput because DbContext instances are reused instead of having new instances created for every request.

Important to note is that the key we used for our connection string in the appsettings.json file must match the string passed to the GetConnectionString method.

Now that we have registered the DbContext as a service in the IServiceCollection, we need to make a change to the VideoDbContext class itself. We need to tell it about the connection string we are using as well as any other options specified with the DbContextOptionsBuilder.

Listing 4-10. The Modified VideoDbContext Class

```
using Microsoft.EntityFrameworkCore;
using VideoStore.Core;

namespace VideoStore.Data
{
    public class VideoDbContext : DbContext
    {
        public VideoDbContext(DbContextOptions<VideoDbContext>
        dbContextOptns) : base(dbContextOptns)
        {

        }

        public DbSet<Video> Videos { get; set; }
    }
}
```

We do this by adding a constructor to the VideoDbContext class and passing the DbContextOptions as seen in Listing 4-10. Because the VideoDbContext class inherits from DbContext, we simply need to pass the DbContextOptions through to the base class. Looking at the metadata for the DbContext class (Listing 4-11), we can see that it takes the DbContextOptions as a parameter in its constructor.

Listing 4-11. The DbContext Metadata

```
//
// Summary:
//     Initializes a new instance of the
//     Microsoft.EntityFrameworkCore.DbContext class
//     using the specified options. The Microsoft.EntityFrameworkCore
//     .DbContext.OnConfiguring(Microsoft.EntityFrameworkCore
//     .DbContextOptionsBuilder) method will still be called to
```

```
//      allow further configuration of the options.
//
// Parameters:
//   options:
//      The options for this context.
public DbContext([NotNullAttribute] DbContextOptions options);

//
// Summary:
//      Initializes a new instance
//      of the Microsoft.EntityFrameworkCore.DbContext class.
//      The Microsoft.EntityFrameworkCore.DbContext
//      .OnConfiguring(Microsoft.EntityFrameworkCore
//      .DbContextOptionsBuilder)
//      method will be called to configure the database
//      (and other options) to be used for this context.
protected DbContext();
```

What remains now is for us to use database migrations to create the database we specified in the connection string earlier.

Working with Database Migrations

Working with migrations can be easy, and it can be somewhat tricky. I know that this seems a bit contradictory, but hear me out. I am going to add migrations to the VideoStore project using the command line. I had a few hiccups while setting this up, but I'll outline what caused these issues next.

What I want to do is see if I can run the dotnet ef dbcontext info command from the command line as illustrated in Listing 4-12.

Listing 4-12. Getting the DbContext Info

```
dotnet ef dbcontext info
```

I should get an error telling me that it can't create the VideoDbContext, and this is expected.

If you receive an error stating that the dotnet tool can't be found when trying to run dotnet ef dbcontext info, then you might need to install it first. Run dotnet tool install --global dotnet-ef. For more, see the following article: https://docs.microsoft.com/en-us/dotnet/core/tools/dotnet-tool-install.

The reason for this is because the VideoStore.Data project is a separate project. It does not know anything about the Startup.cs class that contains the ConfigureServices method. Remember that we modified this in Listing 4-9 earlier in the chapter.

We, therefore, need to tell .NET Core where the startup project is for our solution. We do this by specifying -s and giving it the path to the startup project's csproj file (Listing 4-13).

.NET Core now knows about the startup project and will be able to find the connection string and DbContext class.

Listing 4-13. Telling .NET Core Where the Startup Project Is

```
dotnet ef dbcontext info -s ..\VideoStore\VideoStore.csproj
```

Running the command shown in Listing 4-13 will produce an output similar to what is illustrated in Listing 4-14.

Listing 4-14. The Expected Output

```
Build started...
Build succeeded.
Provider name: Microsoft.EntityFrameworkCore.SqlServer
Database name: VideoStore
Data source: (localdb)\MSSQLLocalDB
Options: MaxPoolSize=128
```

It is here that I also ran into a strange error. It was, unfortunately, as a result of my ignorance. When trying to run the command in Listing 3-13 earlier, I received an error stating that the startup project didn't include Microsoft.EntityFrameworkCore.Design NuGet package (Figure 4-6).

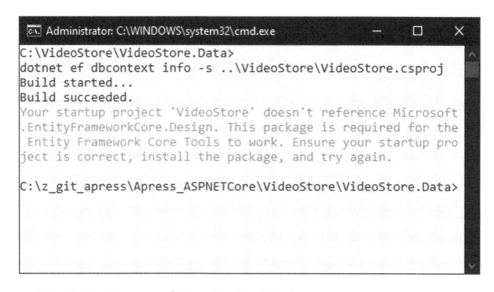

Figure 4-6. *EntityFrameworkCore.Design Missing*

I went ahead and installed that from NuGet and tried adding the migrations again. This time I received this error in Listing 4-15.

Listing 4-15. Create Method Error

```
Method 'Create' in type 'Microsoft.EntityFrameworkCore.SqlServer.Query.
Internal.SqlServerSqlTranslatingExpressionVisitorFactory' from assembly
'Microsoft.EntityFrameworkCore.SqlServer, Version=3.1.9.0, Culture=neutral,
PublicKeyToken=adb9793829ddae60' does not have an implementation.
```

To cut to the chase, this was as a result of a version mismatch between the EntityFrameworkCore NuGet packages in my VideoStore.Data project and my startup project. You need to ensure that the versions match (as seen in Figure 4-7).

In my case, the version was 3.1.9, but it might be different for you.

It is usually a good idea to ensure that the versions of similar NuGet packages between projects match; otherwise, you could end up chasing an error that wastes time and frustrates you no end.

Finally, we are ready to add the migration to our data project. Migrations allow us to keep our database in sync with our data models as they are modified. Migrations work as follows:

- When a data model changes, you can add a migration to your project that will describe the changes required to keep the database in sync with your project. What EF Core does is compare the current data model to a snapshot of the old model and figure out the differences. Migration files are then generated.

- EF Core will then apply generated migrations to the database and record this history in a table. This allows you to see which migrations have been applied and which haven't.

For more information on migrations, be sure to check out the following article on Microsoft Docs here: `https://docs.microsoft.com/en-us/ef/core/managing-schemas/migrations/?tabs=dotnet-core-cli`.

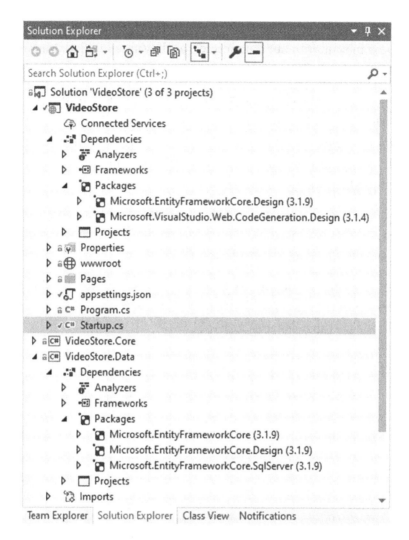

Figure 4-7. *Ensure the Same EntityFrameworkCore Versions*

Let's have a look at some of the options available to us when running `dotnet ef` from the command line.

If you have a look at the output as illustrated in Listing 4-16, you will notice that `migrations` are one of the options.

Listing 4-16. The dotnet ef Command Output

```
Entity Framework Core .NET Command-line Tools 5.0.0

Usage: dotnet ef [options] [command]

Options:
  --version        Show version information
  -h|--help        Show help information
  -v|--verbose     Show verbose output.
  --no-color       Don't colorize output.
  --prefix-output  Prefix output with level.

Commands:
  database    Commands to manage the database.
  dbcontext   Commands to manage DbContext types.
  migrations  Commands to manage migrations.

Use "dotnet ef [command] --help" for more information about a command.
```

Go ahead and run dotnet ef migrations from the command line, and inspect the output as illustrated in Listing 4-17.

Listing 4-17. The dotnet ef migrations Command Output

```
Usage: dotnet ef migrations [options] [command]

Options:
  -h|--help        Show help information
  -v|--verbose     Show verbose output.
  --no-color       Don't colorize output.
  --prefix-output  Prefix output with level.
```

```
Commands:
  add     Adds a new migration.
  list    Lists available migrations.
  remove  Removes the last migration.
  script  Generates a SQL script from migrations.
```

Use "migrations [command] --help" for more information about a command

Here, you will see that we can list all the migrations, remove them, add them, or generate a SQL script from our migrations. In our case, for now, we want to add a new migration.

Run the command as illustrated in Listing 4-18 to add a new migration to our VideoStore.Data project.

Listing 4-18. Add a New Migration

```
dotnet ef migrations add 20201114a -s ..\VideoStore\VideoStore.csproj
```

As before, I am specifying the startup project, but I have also specified a name for the migration file that needs to be generated.

I called my migration file 20201114a as the date and a (denoting the first migration). This is, however, slightly unnecessary as the migration file does include the date. I just prefer to add this to the migration file name, but you can name your migration anything that makes sense to you.

After the migration has been added, the output in your Console Window should be as illustrated in Listing 4-19.

Listing 4-19. Migration Added

```
Build started...
Build succeeded.
Done. To undo this action, use 'ef migrations remove'
```

Going back to Visual Studio, you will notice that .NET Core has added a Migrations folder to your VideoStore.Data project. Inside that folder, you will find your newly added migration (Figure 4-8).

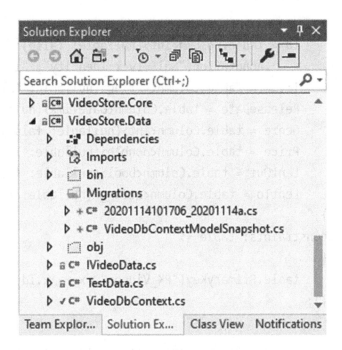

Figure 4-8. *Migrations Added to Visual Studio*

Opening the file in Visual Studio (Listing 4-20), you will see that it simply creates a table called Videos. This is because we have a data model called Video in the VideoStore.Core project.

Listing 4-20. The Generated Migration File

```
using System;
using Microsoft.EntityFrameworkCore.Migrations;

namespace VideoStore.Data.Migrations
{
    public partial class _20201114a : Migration
    {
        protected override void Up(MigrationBuilder migrationBuilder)
        {
            migrationBuilder.CreateTable(
                name: "Videos",
                columns: table => new
```

```
            {
                Id = table.Column<int>(nullable: false)
                    .Annotation("SqlServer:Identity", "1, 1"),
                Title = table.Column<string>(nullable: false),
                ReleaseDate = table.Column<DateTime>(nullable: false),
                Genre = table.Column<int>(nullable: false),
                Price = table.Column<double>(nullable: false),
                LentOut = table.Column<bool>(nullable: false),
                LentTo = table.Column<string>(nullable: true)
            },
            constraints: table =>
            {
                table.PrimaryKey("PK_Videos", x => x.Id);
            });
    }

    protected override void Down(MigrationBuilder migrationBuilder)
    {
        migrationBuilder.DropTable(
            name: "Videos");
    }
  }
}
```

The EF Core migrations saw that there does not exist a table called Videos in the database and generated the code that will create the table for us.

Thinking back to Listing 4-16, you will remember that one of the dotnet ef commands was database. From the command line (while still being in the VideoStore.Data project), run the command as illustrated in Listing 4-21 to create the database for us.

Listing 4-21. Creating the Database

```
dotnet ef database update -s ..\VideoStore\VideosStore.csproj
```

For a few seconds, after the command is run, you will not see much in the Console output. When the process is complete, you will see the output as illustrated in Listing 4-22.

Listing 4-22. Database Creation Completed

```
Build started...
Build succeeded.
Done.
```

We now have a database created for us on our MSSQLLocalDb database instance. Opening up SQL Server Object Explorer in Visual Studio, you will see that the database has been created (Figure 4-9).

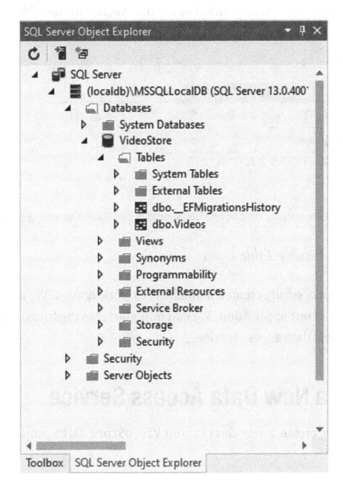

Figure 4-9. *The Database in SQL Server Object Explorer*

Expanding the Tables folder, you will see the Videos table that was created for us.

You can open SQL Server Object Explorer in Visual Studio by going to the View menu and clicking SQL Server Object Explorer or by holding down Ctrl+\, Ctrl+S. Not the most obvious keyboard shortcut, but there it is.

Remember earlier in this chapter, when I said that EF Core will record applied migrations in a history table? You can see that table just above the Videos table, called _EFMigrationsHistory. Right-click the table, and select View Data. You will see a history of migrations, with the one we just added as the only record in the table (Figure 4-10).

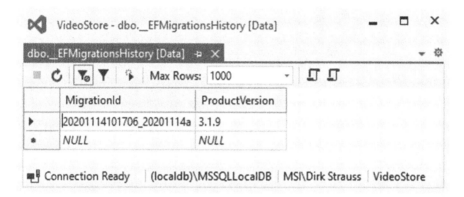

Figure 4-10. *The History Table Data*

We have now successfully created a database to work against. We are finally ready to switch gears inside of our application. We can now start moving from using the TestData service to using a real data access service.

Implement a New Data Access Service

Inside Visual Studio, create a new class in your VideoStore.Data project (Figure 4-11) called SQLData.

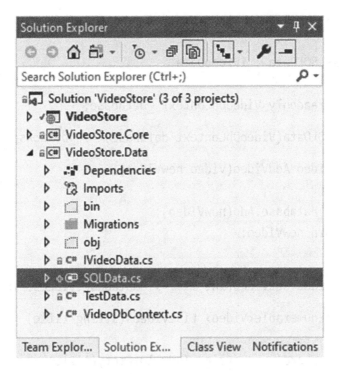

Figure 4-11. *The New SQLData Class*

Make this class implement the IVideoData Interface, and allow Visual Studio to implement the Interface. We now need to add implementations for all the methods specified in the implemented IVideoData Interface.

Take note that you will need to include the System.Linq namespace.

You can see these implementations in Listing 4-23. Using Entity Framework results in less code in some places. Where possible, I have used an expression body for methods as well as the constructor. You are welcome to change this code to use body blocks, but I find expression-bodied members easier to read.

Listing 4-23. The New SQLData Class Implementing IVideoData

```
using Microsoft.EntityFrameworkCore;
using System.Collections.Generic;
using System.Linq;
using VideoStore.Core;
```

```
namespace VideoStore.Data
{
    public class SQLData : IVideoData
    {
        private readonly VideoDbContext _database;

        public SQLData(VideoDbContext database) => _database = database;

        public Video AddVideo(Video newVideo)
        {
            _ = _database.Add(newVideo);
            return newVideo;
        }

        public Video GetVideo(int id) => _database.Videos.Find(id);

        public IEnumerable<Video> ListVideos(string title) => _database.
        Videos
                .Where(x => string.IsNullOrEmpty(title)
                || x.Title.StartsWith(title))
                .OrderBy(x => x.Title);

        public int Save() => _database.SaveChanges();

        public Video UpdateVideo(Video videoData)
        {
            var entity = _database.Videos.Attach(videoData);
            entity.State = EntityState.Modified;
            return videoData;
        }
    }
}
```

Of particular interest, you will notice that I bring in my VideoDbContext via the class constructor and save it to a private field called _database. The AddVideo, GetVideo, and ListVideo methods are self-explanatory, but the UpdateVideo needs to set the EntityState to Modified. This tells the Entity Framework that something on the Video entity has changed.

All that remains for us to do is to swap out the data service in the ConfigureServices method in the Startup.cs class.

Changing the Data Access Service Registration

By changing the data access service registration, we are telling the services collection that whenever something in the application wants to use IVideoData, provide it SQLData. The change in the ConfigureServices method is small and quick. You can see that change in Listing 4-24.

Listing 4-24. The Modified Data Access Service Registration

```
public void ConfigureServices(IServiceCollection services)
{
    _ = services.AddDbContextPool<VideoDbContext>(dbContextOptns =>
    {
        _ = dbContextOptns.UseSqlServer(
            Configuration.GetConnectionString("VideoConn"));
    });

    _ = services.AddScoped<IVideoData, SQLData>();
    _ = services.AddRazorPages().AddSessionStateTempDataProvider();
    _ = services.AddSession();
}
```

We have also defined it to use a scoped lifetime. With everything added, we can now run the application, and we will see no videos listed in our Video List.

This is because we have swapped out the service to use the SQL database, and the Videos table is currently empty. To add a new video, click the add button and add a new video. After adding the new video, return to the list of videos to see the newly added entry (Figure 4-12).

I know some of you are reeling in horror because I added *The Lord of the Rings* as an action movie. Seeing *The Lord of the Rings* as a trilogy, the title should probably also change. Currently, we can't delete any videos from the list. I will therefore leave that up to you to implement on the `IVideoData` Interface and provide the implementation for it on the `SQLData` class.

With the newly added video listed in our list of videos, let's go and look at the data in the database table.

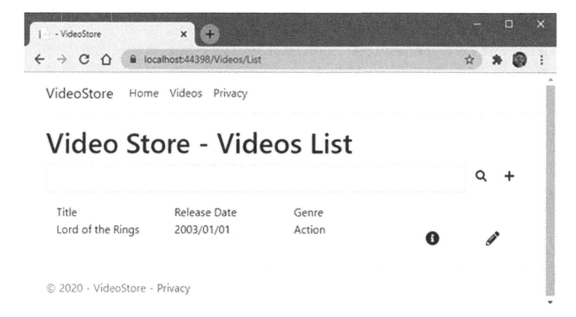

Figure 4-12. *New Video Added to SQL Database*

In the `Videos` table of our `VideoStore` database, you will see the newly added video (Figure 4-13).

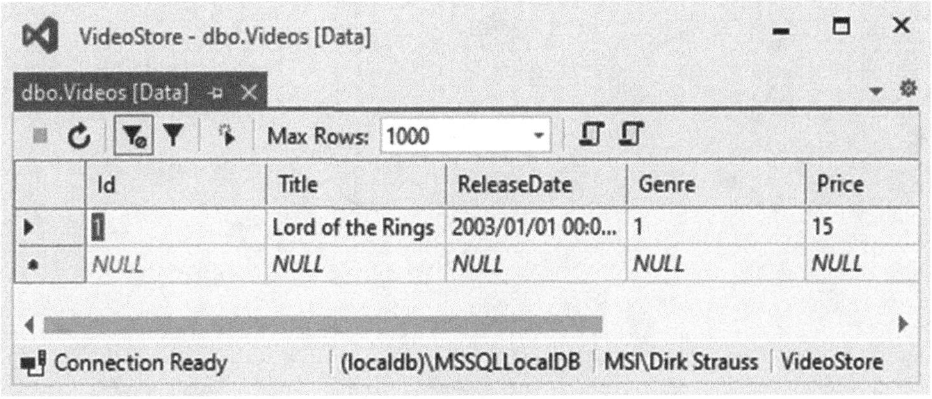

Figure 4-13. *The Added Video in the SQL Table*

This is the power of using interfaces. We have decoupled our data access service and allowed it to implement the IVideoData Interface instead. We can now create a new class, for example, that needs to generate a JSON file with video data. Sure, this will require a lot of string manipulation and probably isn't the best place for storing our video data, but the concept is sound. As long as our data service (any data service) implements the IVideoData Interface, we will be able to inject it into our services collection in the ConfigureServices method.

We will also easily be able to swap out the service for a different one, should the need arise.

CHAPTER 5

Working with Razor Pages

In this chapter, you will learn about working with the UI. Here, we will see how _ViewImports and _ViewStart files work. We will look at partial views and ViewComponents and see what sections in Razor pages can do. The most important thing to realize is that you don't have to be a whizz kid with UI design to create a nice looking, user-friendly UI.

With Bootstrap and a little bit of jQuery, developers can create functional, responsive, and great-looking web UIs for their applications.

Using Sections in Your Razor Pages

If you think back to ASP.NET Master Pages, you will have an idea of what the _Layout. cshtml page (Figure 5-1) is used for. By convention, this page starts with an underscore. It is used to define the structure of your pages and is broken up into a header, body, and footer. The abbreviated code listing for the _Layout.cshtml page is illustrated in Listing 5-1.

Listing 5-1. The _Layout.cshtml Page

```
<!DOCTYPE html>
<html lang="en">
<head>
    @* Meta Tags and CSS *@
</head>
<body>
    <header>
        @* Navigation *@
    </header>
```

149

© Dirk Strauss 2021
D. Strauss, *Creating ASP.NET Core Web Applications*, https://doi.org/10.1007/978-1-4842-6828-5_5

```
<div class="container">
    <main role="main" class="pb-3">
        @RenderBody()
    </main>
</div>

<footer class="border-top footer text-muted">
    @* Footer *@
</footer>

@* Scripts applied across all pages *@

@RenderSection("Scripts", required: false)
</body>
</html>
```

The _Layout page is usually found in the Shared folder by convention.

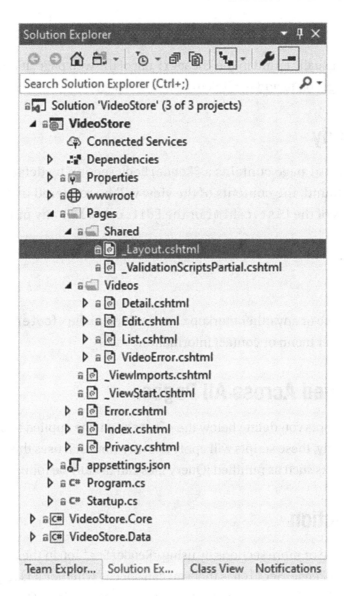

Figure 5-1. *The _Layout.cshtml Page*

Let's have a look at the different areas in the _Layout page.

Meta Tags and CSS

Meta tags and links to CSS files are added to the <head> tags on a web page. It is here that you would add links to the minified Bootstrap CSS or your custom CSS files, for example.

Navigation

The navigation is usually found in the `<header>` tag of the web page. It is here that we modified the navigation to add the link to the Videos page.

@RenderBody

The `_Layout.cshtml` page contains a `@RenderBody` section by default. Wherever the `@RenderBody` is found, the contents of the view will be rendered in it. This means that the contents of the `List.cshtml` or the `Edit.cshtml` or any other view are rendered here.

Footer

The copyright notice or any other markup can be added to the `<footer>` section. Some sites include a footer menu or contact information.

Scripts Applied Across All Pages

The links to the scripts you define below the `<footer>` will be applied to all pages on the site. More accurately, these scripts will apply to every view that uses this specific layout page. Links to scripts such as minified jQuery files can usually be found here.

@RenderSection

Layouts can call one or more sections by using `@RenderSection` in the markup. The nice thing about using `@RenderSection` is that you can specify whether it is required or not. In Listing 5-1, you will notice that the `Scripts` section is not required. Open up the `List.cshtml` page, and add the code in Listing 5-2 at the end of the page.

Listing 5-2. Added Scripts Section to List Page

```
@section Scripts {
    <script>
        $(document).ready(function () {
            alert("I am a script alert");
        });
    </script>
}
```

Notice that the name of the section, Scripts, must match the name supplied in the @ RenderSection call. Run your web application, and open the Video List page. You should see a pop-up displayed as illustrated in Figure 5-2.

Figure 5-2. *The Script Alert*

From the list of videos, click one to view the details. When the Detail page loads, no script is displayed. This is because no Scripts section exists on the Detail.cshtml page, and we have told the _Layout.cshtml file that the Scripts section is not required.

Modify the @RenderSection on the _Layout.cshtml page as illustrated in Listing 5-3.

Listing 5-3. Modified RenderSection

```
@RenderSection("Scripts", required: true)
```

If you run your web app again, you will receive an error because you have told ASP. NET Core that the Scripts section is mandatory, but you have not included a Scripts section as illustrated in Listing 5-2 on every page on your site.

This is, in essence, how you can render sections in your web application. The @ RenderSection isn't just good for scripts. It can contain markup too. Go back to the _Layout.cshtml page, and add the following code as illustrated in Listing 5-4 just below the closing </header> tag.

Listing 5-4. Notification Section

```
@RenderSection("Notification", required: false)
```

Switch back to your List.cshtml page, and add the code illustrated in Listing 5-5 to the bottom of the page.

Listing 5-5. Notification Section

```
@section Notification {
<div class="row">
    <div class="col-md-12 alert alert-info">
        This is a notification
    </div>
</div>
}
```

Run the web application again, and have a look at the Video List page. You will see the notification displayed at the top of the page below the navigation (Figure 5-3).

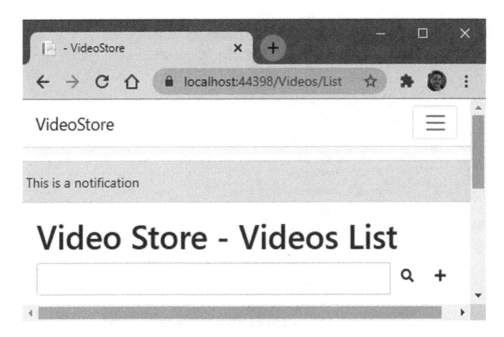

Figure 5-3. *The Displayed Notification Section*

Interesting to note is that while the markup was added to the bottom of the List. cshtml page, it did not affect where the markup was displayed on the rendered page. The Notification section is displayed exactly where the @RenderSection was positioned on the _Layout.cshtml page. Sections, therefore, allow you to easily plug in additional markup or logic into your Razor pages. This allows you to easily structure your page elements and organize where they should go.

What Are _ViewImports and _ViewStart Files?

So far, we have spoken a bit about layout pages. At the beginning of this chapter, we said that thinking back to ASP.NET Master Pages will give you an idea of what the _Layout. cshtml page is used for. It is applied to all your views, and in our sample application, this would be the pages we created for our application.

How exactly does each page (or view) know to use the _Layout.cshtml page? This is where the _ViewStart.cshtml page comes into play (Figure 5-4).

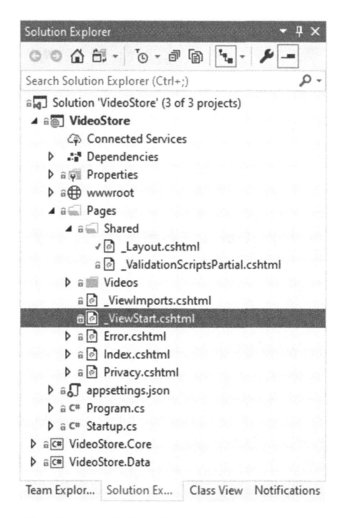

Figure 5-4. *The _ViewStart and _ViewImports Pages*

By default, before a page is rendered in your web application, ASP.NET Core will check the _ViewStart page to see what layout page it should apply. You can see the markup for the _ViewStart page in Listing 5-6 specifies that the application must use the _Layout page when rendering a page.

Listing 5-6. The _ViewStart Markup

```
@{
    Layout = "_Layout";
}
```

What if you need to apply a different layout for a particular page? Well, as it turns out, you can control exactly what layout page your view uses.

Specifying a Different Layout Page

To test this, create a new Razor page without a Page Model in your Shared folder (Figure 5-5). Call this page _LayoutSpecial, and just copy the markup from the _Layout page and paste it into the _LayoutSpecial page.

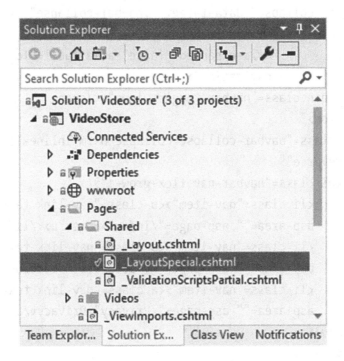

Figure 5-5. *The Newly Added _LayoutSpecial Page*

The reason for using a different layout page is because we want to structure a specific page differently from the default. So to make the _LayoutSpecial page different, I just added a heading on the layout page in the <header> section as seen in Listing 5-7.

Listing 5-7. Modified _LayoutSpecial Page

```
<header>
  <nav class="navbar navbar-expand-sm navbar-toggleable-sm navbar-light bg-
  white border-bottom box-shadow mb-3">
      <div class="container">
          <a class="navbar-brand" asp-area="" asp-page="/Index">
          VideoStore</a>
          <button class="navbar-toggler" type="button" data-
          toggle="collapse" data-target=".navbar-collapse" aria-
          controls="navbarSupportedContent"
                      aria-expanded="false" aria-label="Toggle
                      navigation">
              <span class="navbar-toggler-icon"></span>
          </button>
          <div class="navbar-collapse collapse d-sm-inline-flex flex-sm-
          row-reverse">
              <ul class="navbar-nav flex-grow-1">
                  <li class="nav-item"><a class="nav-link text-dark"
                  asp-area="" asp-page="/Index">Home</a></li>
                  <li class="nav-item"><a class="nav-link text-dark"
                  asp-area="" asp-page="/Videos/List">Videos</a></li>
                  <li class="nav-item"><a class="nav-link text-dark"
                  asp-area="" asp-page="/Privacy">Privacy</a></li>
              </ul>
          </div>
      </div>
  </nav>
  <div class="col-md-12 alert alert-info">
      <h1>
          This is the Special Layout Page
      </h1>
  </div>
</header>
```

You will notice that it still has all the navigation from the _Layout page, but that it now also includes this <h1> element.

Use cases for a different layout page will differ, but consider the requirement to apply a different layout based on whether the user is logged in or not. Perhaps you need to apply a notification banner to a specific page only.

Now let's apply this _LayoutSpecial page to the Detail view. Open up the Detail. cshtml file, and add the code as illustrated in Listing 5-8 to the Detail page.

Listing 5-8. Specifying a Different Layout Page

```
@page "{videoId:int}"
@model VideoStore.Pages.Videos.DetailModel
@{
    ViewData["Title"] = "Detail";
    Layout = "_LayoutSpecial";
}
```

When ASP.NET Core finds the Layout = "_LayoutSpecial" in the header of the Detail page, it then goes out and looks for that layout page in the Shared folder. It then applies that specific layout only to the Detail page. If you run the application and navigate to the Detail page, you will see the heading applied as illustrated in Figure 5-6.

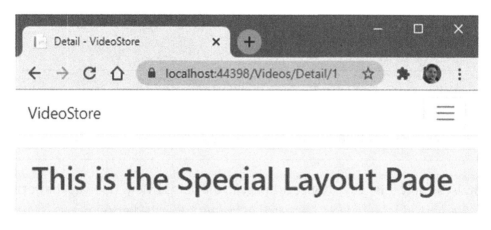

Figure 5-6. *The New Layout Applied to the Detail Page*

So the _ViewStart page plays an important role in ASP.NET Core. In the preceding example, it specified the layout page to apply to all views in the application. We saw how we can override the default layout, by specifying a different layout for a particular page. This means that if we need to run code before each view, we need to place it in the _ViewStart file. By convention, _ViewStart is located in the Pages folder and is hierarchical. In other words, if another _ViewStart is found in a subfolder, it will be run after the _ViewStart in the root folder.

Note that some name the Pages folder Views. Whatever your preference, the term page and view are used interchangeably.

Another file to take note of is the _ViewImports file. Let's have a look at what it does in a bit more detail.

Creating a Custom TagHelper

The code for the _ViewImports file is illustrated in Listing 5-9.

Listing 5-9. The _ViewImports File

```
@using VideoStore
@namespace VideoStore.Pages
@addTagHelper *, Microsoft.AspNetCore.Mvc.TagHelpers
```

This file uses Razor directives to import namespaces that need to be shared by other views. The following directives are supported in the _ViewImports file:

- @addTagHelper

- @removeTagHelper

- @tagHelperPrefix

- @using

- @model

- @inherits

- @inject

Like the _ViewStart file, the _ViewImports file is hierarchical, and if multiple _ViewImports.cshtml files are found in that hierarchy, the directives are combined as follows:

- All @addTagHelper and @removeTagHelper directives are run in order.

- The closest @tagHelperPrefix to the view will override any others.

- The closest @model to the view will override any others.

- The closest @inherits to the view will override any others.

- All @using directives are included, and any duplicates are ignored.

- For every @inject property, the closest one to the view will override any others with the same property names.

The _ViewImports file is also the place where you will define any custom tag helpers you may create. Have a look at the Detail page markup again (Listing 5-10).

Listing 5-10. The Price Markup

```
<div>
    Price: $@Model.Video.Price
</div>
```

Here, we can see that the currency is hardcoded into the markup of the page. This is not something we want to do and generally does not scale well. Let's create a custom tag helper to get the currency as defined by the culture name we pass it.

To do this, we are going to do the following:

- Add a folder for our custom tag helpers.

- Add a class for the tag helper for video price.

- Specify our custom tag helper in the _ViewImports file.

You can see that we have added a new folder to the solution called TagHelpers (Figure 5-7). We have also added a class called PriceTagHelper to the TagHelpers folder.

This class will tell the compiler that it should match all videoPrice elements and look for attributes that match video-price and culture-name. The class will then get the currency symbol for the culture name you pass it and output the price with the correct currency symbol.

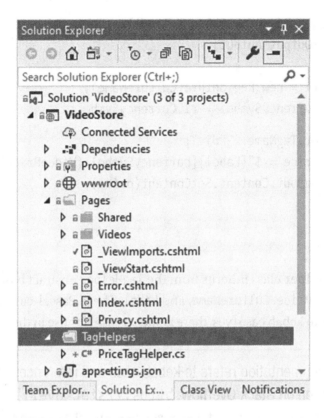

Figure 5-7. *Add the TagHelper Folder and Class*

Start by creating a class named PriceTagHelper in the TagHelpers folder. You can see the complete code listing illustrated in Listing 5-11.

Listing 5-11. The PriceTagHelper Class

```
using Microsoft.AspNetCore.Razor.TagHelpers;
using System.Globalization;

namespace VideoStore.TagHelpers
{
    [HtmlTargetElement("videoPrice")]
    public class PriceTagHelper : TagHelper
    {
        public double VideoPrice { get; set; }
        public string CultureName { get; set; }
        public string Label { get; set; }
```

```
        public override void Process(TagHelperContext context,
        TagHelperOutput output)
        {
            var ri = new RegionInfo(CultureName);
            var currencySymbol = ri.CurrencySymbol;

            output.TagName = "div";
            var price = $"{Label}{currencySymbol}{VideoPrice}";
            _ = output.Content.SetContent(price);
        }
    }
}
```

The PriceTagHelper class inherits from the TagHelper abstract base class. It defines properties for VideoPrice, CultureName, and Label. These Pascal-cased property names will be translated into kebab case (yes, there is such a case) for use in the markup attributes.

The Microsoft Documentation refers to kebab case and references the following discussion on Stack Overflow: https://stackoverflow.com/questions/11273282/whats-the-name-for-hyphen-separated-case/12273101#12273101.

Note that this class is in the VideoStore.TagHelpers namespace. We will, therefore, need to declare only the VideoStore namespace in the _ViewImports file as seen in Listing 5-12.

Listing 5-12. Adding the Custom Tag Helper

```
@using VideoStore
@namespace VideoStore.Pages
@addTagHelper *, Microsoft.AspNetCore.Mvc.TagHelpers

@addTagHelper *, VideoStore
```

Looking back at the code in Listing 5-11, you will see that the class has an HtmlTargetElement attribute telling the compiler to target all videoPrice elements. With this, all in place, build your project and modify the Detail page markup.

Looking back at Listing 5-10, you will remember that we hardcoded the currency. With our custom tag helper in place, we can simply add the markup listed in Listing 5-13.

Listing 5-13. The New Video Price Markup Using a Custom Tag Helper

```
<videoPrice video-price="@Model.Video.Price" culture-name="en-GB"
label="Price: "></videoPrice>
```

The custom tag helper uses the culture you pass it to determine the currency symbol to display. It also allows you to specify a label for the video price. As mentioned earlier, it uses these attributes (`video-price`, `culture-name`, and `label`) to map to the properties of the `PriceTagHelper` class.

Working with Partial Views

I generally assume that .NET developers think in an object-oriented manner. At least, I do, and this is why I think the concept of partial views will be quite easy to grasp. The definition of a partial view according to the Microsoft Documentation explains it quite nicely.

> *A partial view is a Razor markup file (.cshtml) without an @page directive that renders HTML output within another markup file's rendered output.*

This means that the partial view only renders as a part of your content which is very useful when breaking up large complex views into smaller, more manageable pieces. This also makes it a fantastic way to reduce the duplication of markup across files.

In the Solution Explorer, go ahead and add a partial view to your `Videos` folder by right-clicking the folder and clicking `Add` and then `Razor Page` from the context menu. Select `Razor Page` from the `Add New Scaffolded Item` dialog that is displayed, and click the `Add` button.

I feel that the process of adding a partial view can be streamlined a lot in Visual Studio. Nevertheless, the process is currently the way it is.

From the `Add Razor Page` dialog that is displayed, only check the `Create as a partial view` check box as seen in Figure 5-8.

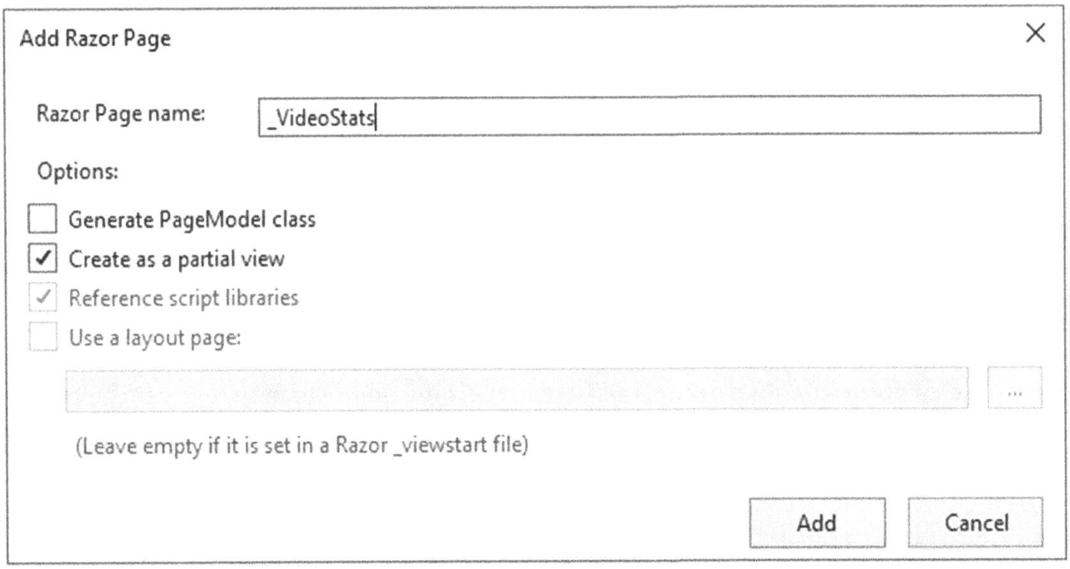

Figure 5-8. *Adding the _VideoStats Partial View*

Name the partial view _VideoStats, and click the Add button. You should see your partial view as illustrated in Figure 5-9. This partial view will contain the following information on each video:

- A rating

- A short review

- A URL for the video online

To make this possible, we need to digress a little bit and move away from the partial view creation. We will need to add these properties to our Video class in the VideoStore. Core project.

Because the properties are added to our Video class, we must update our database table.

Figure 5-9. *The _VideoStats Added to the Pages Folder*

It is here that the true benefit of migrations becomes obvious. We can quickly update our database with these changes.

Adding Video Properties and Updating the Database

We want to add some statistics to the Video class where we can store the rating, a short review, and a URL to the video. Add the properties in Listing 5-14 to the Video class in the VideoStore.Core project.

Listing 5-14. The New Video Properties

```
public int Rating { get; set; }
public string Review { get; set; }
public string OnlineURL { get; set; }
```

I will not be posting the entire Video class code here, as I am sure you know where to add the additional properties in Listing 5-14. Save the project, and open a Command Prompt in the VideoStore.Data project folder.

In other words, open a Command Prompt, and change the directory to your VideoStore.Data project. You can also right-click the VideoStore.Data project in the Solution Explorer and click Open Folder in File Explorer.

When you have opened the Command Prompt, you are ready to add the new EF Migrations to it by running the command in Listing 5-15.

Listing 5-15. Add New EF Migrations

```
dotnet ef migrations add AddRatings -s ..\VideoStore\VideoStore.csproj
```

The migrations called AddRatings are added to the Migrations folder when the command has run (Figure 5-10).

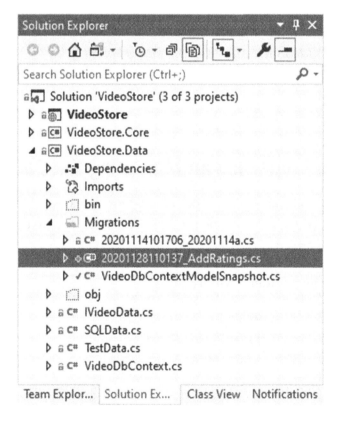

Figure 5-10. *The AddRating Migrations Added*

Next, we need to update the database table which is done by running the command in Listing 5-16.

Listing 5-16. Update the Database

```
dotnet ef database update -s ..\VideoStore\VideoStore.csproj
```

Once this command has run, the Videos table in the VideoStore database in SQL Server Object Explorer will be updated (Figure 5-11).

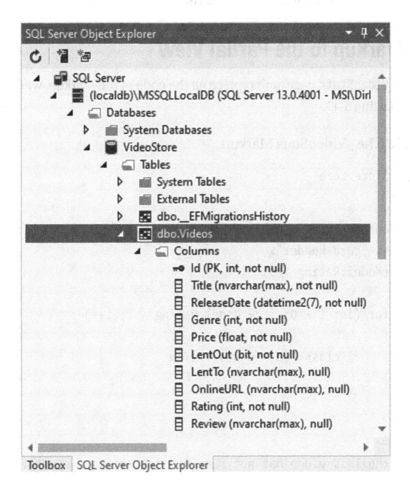

Figure 5-11. *The Updated Videos Table*

We now have added all the necessary parts to get our _VideoStats partial view working.

I have not added any code allowing us to provide values for these properties when adding or editing a video. I will leave this for you as a homework assignment. For now, I will just be adding the data directly to the database table.

To add the data for the additional properties, open SQL Server Object Explorer, and right-click the Videos table. Select View Data from the context menu, and add data for the Rating, Review, and OnlineURL columns.

Adding Markup to the Partial View

Open up the _VideoStats page, and replace all the code in the markup, with the markup illustrated in Listing 5-17.

Listing 5-17. The _VideoStats Markup

```
@using VideoStore.Core
@model Video

<div class="card" style="width: 18rem;">
    <div class="card-header">
        @if (Model.Rating > 0)
        {
            for (int i = 0; i <= Model.Rating - 1; i++)
            {
                <i class="fas fa-star"></i>
            }
        }
        else
        {
            <h6>This video has not received any ratings yet</h6>
        }
    </div>
    <div class="card-body">
        <h5 class="card-title">@Model.Title</h5>
        <p class="card-text">@Model.Review</p>
```

```
        <a href="@Model.OnlineURL" class="btn btn-primary">View Online</a>
    </div>
</div>
```

This basically just creates a card displaying the additional video statistics. It includes the VideoStore.Core namespace and uses the Video model to display the additional properties we added.

We want to add the video stats card to the Detail.cshtml page. To do this, I want to format the Detail page slightly.

The structure of the Detail page will be as illustrated in Listing 5-18. The page will be divided up into a grid pattern, using div elements.

Listing 5-18. The New Detail Page Structure

```
<div class="row">
    <div class="col-md-12">Title</div>
</div>
<div class="row">
    <div class="col-md-6">Video Details</div>
    <div class="col-md-6">Video Stats</div>
</div>
<div class="row">
    <div class="col-md-12">footer</div>
</div>
```

The top row will contain the video title. The middle row will be further divided into two parts. The left part will contain the existing video details, and the right part will contain our new partial view. The bottom row will be the footer and contain the existing back button that takes us back to the list of videos.

In order to use the partial view in our page, we need to add the partial tag helper. As seen in Listing 5-19, it contains a name which is the name we gave to the partial view, as well as the model we are passing to the partial view.

Listing 5-19. The Partial Tag Helper

```
<partial name="_VideoStats" model="Model.Video" />
```

We can now shuffle all the elements around and plug them into the new Detail page structure. The complete Detail page markup is illustrated in Listing 5-20.

Listing 5-20. The Complete Detail Page

```
@page "{videoId:int}"
@model VideoStore.Pages.Videos.DetailModel
@{
    ViewData["Title"] = "Detail";
    Layout = "_LayoutSpecial";
}

<div class="row">
    <div class="col-md-12"><h1>@Model.Video.Title</h1></div>
</div>
<div class="row">
    <div class="col-md-6">
        @if (Model.CommitMessage != null)
        {
            <div class="alert alert-info">@Model.CommitMessage</div>
        }

        <div>
            Catalog ID: @Model.Video.Id
        </div>
        <div>
            Release Date: @Model.Video.ReleaseDate.ToString("dd MMMM yyyy")
        </div>
        <div>
            Genre: @Model.Video.Genre
        </div>
        <videoPrice video-price="@Model.Video.Price" culture-name="en-GB"
        label="Price: "></videoPrice>
        <div>
            Lent Out: @Html.CheckBoxFor(x => x.Video.LentOut)
        </div>
```

```
    @if (Model.Video.LentOut == true)
    {
        <div>
            Lent To: @Model.Video.LentTo
        </div>
    }
    </div>
    <div class="col-md-6">
        <partial name="_VideoStats" model="Model.Video" />
    </div>
</div>
<div class="row">
    <div class="col-md-12"><a asp-page="./List" class="btn btn-outline-
    primary">Back to Videos</a></div>
</div>
```

When this is complete, build and run your project. The Detail page is displayed as in Figure 5-12.

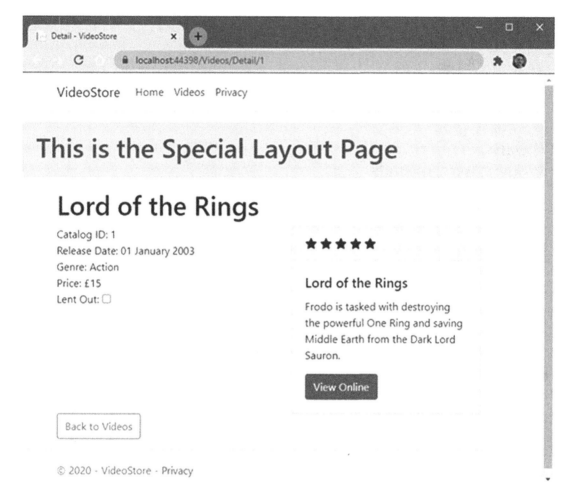

Figure 5-12. *The Modified Detail Page*

The Detail page is split in two, with the video stats displayed on the right half of the page. You can simplify the Detail page even further by adding another partial view called _VideoDetail to the Videos folder.

I will leave this for you to complete as an exercise, but the code accompanying this book contains the completed logic. What you want to end up with is a Detail page that looks as illustrated in Listing 5-21.

Listing 5-21. The Simplified Detail Page

```
@page "{videoId:int}"
@model VideoStore.Pages.Videos.DetailModel
@{
    ViewData["Title"] = "Detail";
    Layout = "_LayoutSpecial";
}

<div class="row">
    <div class="col-md-12"><h1>@Model.Video.Title</h1></div>
</div>
<div class="row">
    <div class="col-md-6">
        @if (Model.CommitMessage != null)
        {
            <div class="alert alert-info">@Model.CommitMessage</div>
        }
        <partial name="_VideoDetail" model="Model.Video" />
    </div>
    <div class="col-md-6">
        <partial name="_VideoStats" model="Model.Video" />
    </div>
</div>
<div class="row">
    <div class="col-md-12"><a asp-page="./List" class="btn btn-outline-
primary">Back to Videos</a></div>
</div>
```

Partial views are perfect for simplifying complex or large markup and allows for easy reuse of components in your markup.

Working with ViewComponents

So far in this chapter, we have looked at sections, _ViewImports, _ViewStart, and partial views. With partial views, we saw that we can pass it a model to use, and in the previous example, we passed it our Video model. But what if we didn't want to do this? What if we needed to add some type of markup to every page that needed to display some data? Assume that we wanted to add a video of the day section to every page on the site.

When we want to render some markup on every page, we know that we can do this by adding some logic to the _Layout page. This way, we can display the markup on every page that implements that specific layout page. The only problem is that the layout page does not contain a page model. It has no way of accessing any data, and we want to access some data to display on every page in our Video Store.

This is where the view components come into play. The view component will be able to function on its own and be able to access data without relying on the Razor page passing it some data.

Start by adding a folder to your VideoStore project called ViewComponents as seen in Figure 5-13.

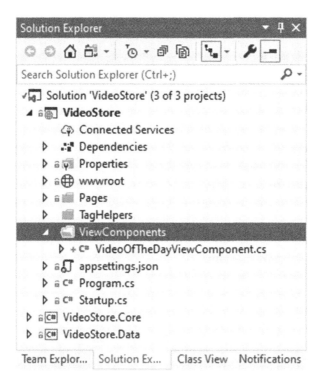

Figure 5-13. *The ViewComponents Folder*

Inside that folder, add a class called VideoOfTheDayViewComponent, and add the code in Listing 5-22.

Listing 5-22. The VideoOfTheDayViewComponent Class

```
using Microsoft.AspNetCore.Mvc;
using VideoStore.Data;

namespace VideoStore.ViewComponents
{
    public class VideoOfTheDayViewComponent : ViewComponent
    {
        private readonly IVideoData _videoData;

        public VideoOfTheDayViewComponent(IVideoData videoData)
        {
            _videoData = videoData;
        }

        public IViewComponentResult Invoke()
        {
            var video = _videoData.GetTopVideo();
            return View(video);
        }
    }
}
```

It is important to note that view components do not respond to HTTP requests. You can think of the view component as a type of partial view that is embedded inside different views on your site. When this view is generated, ASP.NET Core will call a method called Invoke and return an IViewComponentResult to the page.

You must add the VideoStore.Data and Microsoft.AspNetCore.Mvc namespaces to the VideoOfTheDayViewComponent class.

The view component can have a constructor, and it is here that we inject the IVideoData service via dependency injection. This allows the view component to work autonomously with the data in our project. The Invoke method then calls a method on the data service called GetTopVideo.

We must now add this method to our data service. Open up the IVideoData Interface, and add the GetTopVideo method to the Interface as illustrated in Listing 5-23.

Listing 5-23. The Modified IVideoData Interface

```
using System.Collections.Generic;
using VideoStore.Core;

namespace VideoStore.Data
{
    public interface IVideoData
    {
        IEnumerable<Video> ListVideos(string title);
        Video GetVideo(int id);
        Video GetTopVideo();
        Video UpdateVideo(Video videoData);
        Video AddVideo(Video newVideo);
        int Save();
    }
}
```

The GetTopVideo method just returns a Video object. Because the TestData and SQLData classes implement the IVideoData Interface, we need to add implementations to these classes for the GetTopVideo method. I'm not too worried about the implementation for the TestData class, so I'll simply return the first video as seen in Listing 5-24.

Listing 5-24. The TestData Class Implementation

```
public Video GetTopVideo()
{
    return _videoList.First();
}
```

When it comes to the SQLData class, however, I want to be a bit more specific with the code. You can implement the code as you see fit, but I will simply generate a random number between 1 and the count of videos and find the video with that ID.

To be quite honest, the Random class is not truly random. For true randomness, think about implementing a cryptographic random number generator if true randomness is important to you. Jon Skeet has a great article online regarding this. Secondly, one would probably not implement a video of the day using a random ID. You would probably do this using other criteria such as the top 10 rated movies in the Video Store or the most popular videos determined by how many times it has been rented. In any event, I am just trying to explain a concept here of view components. I am not explaining the best way to determine which video is the video of the day.

The code in Listing 5-25 illustrates the implementation of the GetTopVideo method in the SQLData class.

Listing 5-25. The SQLData Class Implementation

```
public Video GetTopVideo()
{
    var rnd = new Random();
    if (_database.Videos.Count() == 0)
        return new Video();
    else
    {
        var r = rnd.Next(1, _database.Videos.Count());
        return _database.Videos.Find(r);
    }}
```

The code is rather simple, so I will not spend too much time explaining it. Next, we need to add a view that will display our video of the day. This is because, referring back to Listing 5-22, we return a View(video) from the Invoke method. View components also follow a very specific naming convention. The _Layout page will be using our video of the day view, so we will be adding it to the Shared folder.

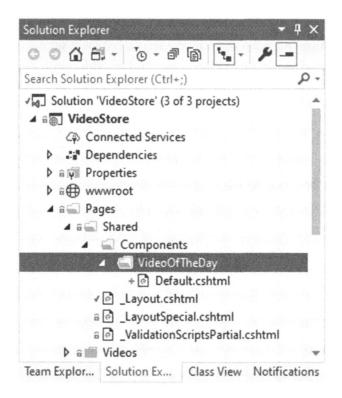

Figure 5-14. *The VideoOfTheDay View*

For ASP.NET Core to be able to locate view component views, I need to create a folder called Components, and inside the Components folder, I need to add another folder called the same as the ViewComponent name, just without the ViewComponent bit on the end. This means that I simply need to call my folder VideoOfTheDay. Inside the VideoOfTheDay folder, I can add views dedicated to my view component.

If you think back to the Invoke method on the VideoOfTheDayViewComponent class, I just returned View(video). I could also have returned View("TodaysVideo", video) by passing the name of the view (TodaysVideo) to return. I would then need to create a view in the VideoOfTheDay folder called TodaysVideo.cshtml. That isn't something I want to do, so I can simply just call my view Default.cshtml as seen in Figure 5-14.

Note that the Default.cshtml page doesn't contain a page model. It's just a regular cshtml file.

We now want to add some markup to the Default.cshtml page. As seen in Listing 5-26, this will remind you about the partial view we created earlier in the chapter.

Listing 5-26. The Default ViewComponent View

```
@using VideoStore.Core
@model Video

<div class="row alert alert-info">
    <div class="col-md-12">
        Video of the day: @Model.Title
    </div>
</div>
```

With this in place, we almost have everything we need.

Usually, at this point, we would need to add the tag helpers in our VideoStore namespace to the _ViewImports file. Because we added a custom tag helper earlier in the chapter, we don't need to do this now.

Back in the _Layout.cshtml page, we can use the vc: tag helper to display the ViewComponent we just created (Listing 5-27) and refer to the name of our view component, in kebab case, without the ViewComponent bit on the end.

Listing 5-27. The vc Tag Helper for Our ViewComponent

```
<vc:video-of-the-day></vc:video-of-the-day>
```

If your project is built, the video-of-the-day tag helper will pop up via IntelliSense. Placing this here tells the tag helper to find a view called VideoOfTheDay and render it.

I just placed this in the footer of my layout page and ran the application. The video of the day will be displayed in the footer of every page as seen in Figure 5-15.

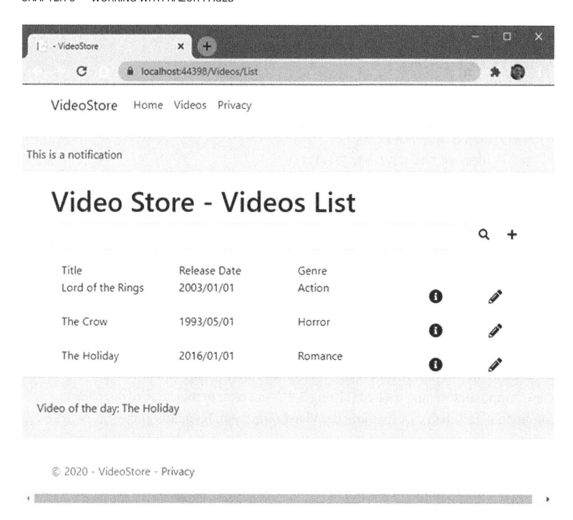

Figure 5-15. *The Video of the Day ViewComponent*

ViewComponents allow you to add logic to your Razor pages while separating the complexity of the code away from the Razor pages. This is because the ViewComponent can access the data on its own. This differs from the partial view that relies on the parent Razor view for the model information.

CHAPTER 6

Adding Client-Side Logic

Part of developing web applications is knowing how to style your UI properly. Some might argue that this is the role of a front-end or full-stack developer, but it is good that every developer knows the basics of CSS, jQuery, and JavaScript.

In this chapter, we will have a look at working with SCSS to create CSS. We will also have a look at using jQuery and JavaScript. Being able to develop client-side logic to add functionality to your web application is a skill web developers need to embrace.

Separate Production Scripts from Development Scripts

During development, it is preferable to be able to separate scripts and other static files from the files that will be used during production. This is important because in a production environment, you might want to use a minified file or a file from a CDN.

Static files are files that are used for Bootstrap, jQuery, fonts, .css, .js, or images. By default, static files are served from the wwwroot folder in your project.

It is possible to tell ASP.NET Core that you want to apply different files in a production environment by using a special tag helper in your markup. We saw in earlier chapters that we could use the _Layout page to apply a specific look and feel to all pages on your site. We also saw that we could override the default _Layout page on certain pages.

A general rule of thumb is that .css files are added in the <head> tags of your _Layout page, while .js files are added last, after the <footer> in the _Layout page. It, therefore, makes sense to control which files are served during development as opposed to production, from the _Layout page.

© Dirk Strauss 2021

D. Strauss, *Creating ASP.NET Core Web Applications*, https://doi.org/10.1007/978-1-4842-6828-5_6

To implement this, we will use the `environment` tag helper. Let's test the use of this special tag helper by adding the code in Listing 6-1 to the `<footer>` section of the _Layout page.

Listing 6-1. Using the Environment Tag Helper

```
<footer class="border-top footer text-muted">
    <vc:video-of-the-day></vc:video-of-the-day>
    <div class="container">
        &copy; 2020 - VideoStore - <a asp-area="" asp-page=
        "/Privacy">Privacy</a>
    </div>

    <environment include="Development">
        <h2>Development</h2>
    </environment>
    <environment exclude="Development">
        <h2>Production</h2>
    </environment>
```

```
</footer>
```

The `include` and `exclude` attributes on the `environment` tag helpers tell ASP.NET Core when to apply the markup contained. In other words, `include="Development"` will only apply the code contained in the `environment` element when you are running a development profile. The opposite is true for the `exclude="Development"` attribute.

To control the profile that you are currently running, open up the `launchSettings.json` file contained in the `Properties` folder of your application. You will see the JSON as illustrated in Listing 6-2.

Listing 6-2. The launchSettings.json File

```
{
  "iisSettings": {
    "windowsAuthentication": false,
    "anonymousAuthentication": true,
    "iisExpress": {
      "applicationUrl": "http://localhost:57104",
```

```
      "sslPort": 44398
    }
  },
  "profiles": {
    "IIS Express": {
      "commandName": "IISExpress",
      "launchBrowser": true,
      "environmentVariables": {
        "ASPNETCORE_ENVIRONMENT": "Development"
      }
    },
    "VideoStore": {
      "commandName": "Project",
      "launchBrowser": true,
      "applicationUrl": "https://localhost:5001;http://localhost:5000",
      "environmentVariables": {
        "ASPNETCORE_ENVIRONMENT": "Development"
      }
    }
  }
}
```

You will notice that we have an IIS Express profile that sets an environment variable called ASPNETCORE_ENVIRONMENT to Development.

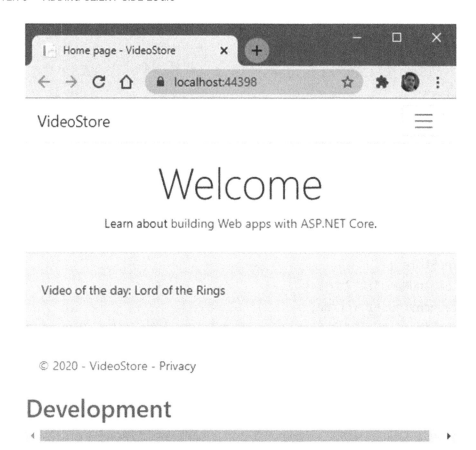

Figure 6-1. *Running the Application in Development*

This means that whenever we launch our application in IIS Express, this profile will be loaded and the environment variable applied. The environment tag helper in the footer then checks this variable and applies the markup applicable to the profile used. Running your application, you will see that the heading Development is displayed as seen in Figure 6-1.

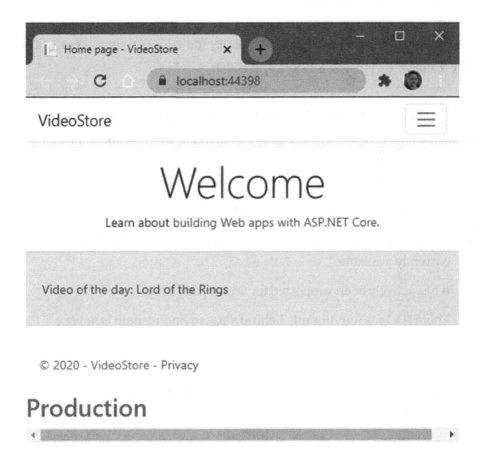

Figure 6-2. *Running the Application in Production*

Back in the launchSettings.json file, change the ASPNETCORE_ENVIRONMENT value to Production and run the application again. You will see that the footer now contains the heading Production (Figure 6-2).

The second profile is called VideoStore, and this profile is used when you run the application from the Console using the dotnet run command. With what we know about the profiles and environment variables, we can easily apply different scripts and styles to our site, based on whether we are running in development or production.

Setting Up SCSS and Generating CSS

Part of styling your application correctly will invariably require developers to use CSS. If you have to use CSS, you will most likely love working with Sass.

Sass is a feature-rich CSS extension language. You can read up more about Sass from the website `https://sass-lang.com/`.

Sass is compatible with all versions of CSS and is widely adopted. It allows developers to create CSS by using the Sass syntax that is then compiled into CSS. It will also create a minified CSS file.

There are many reasons you can use Sass with confidence. Here are a few of them:

- It is compatible with all versions of CSS.

- It boasts more features and abilities than other CSS extensions currently available.

- It has actively been supported for around 14 years.

- There is a large community behind Sass, so finding help is never a problem.

Sass supports features such as variables, nesting, partials, modules, mixins, extensions, inheritance, as well as operators. The use of it will, therefore, come very natural to developers.

More information on these features is available at the following link: `https://sass-lang.com/guide`.

If you were wondering why the heading of this section mentions SCSS, but that I'm talking about Sass, let me explain. There are two kinds of syntaxes used for Sass. Using .sass files, you will not need to use semicolons and curly braces. Using .scss files, however, do use curly braces and semicolons. It doesn't care about indentation levels or whitespace and is a superset of CSS. In fact, SCSS means Sassy CSS. Therefore, SCSS contains all the features of CSS but has also expanded to include Sass features.

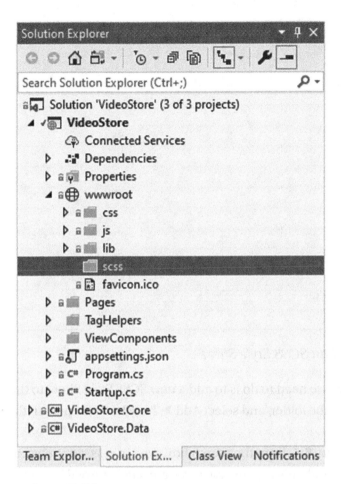

Figure 6-3. *Created scss Folder*

Let's start by creating a folder called scss in the wwwroot of our project. You can see this folder added in Figure 6-3.

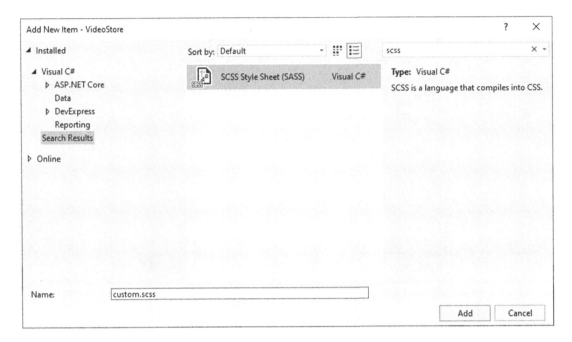

Figure 6-4. *Add an SCSS Style Sheet*

The next thing we need to do is to add a new SCSS Style Sheet to the scss folder. To do this, right-click the folder, and select Add ➤ New Item to open up the Add New Item window.

As seen in Figure 6-4, from the search box, type in scss, and select an SCSS Style Sheet (SASS) file. Call this file custom.scss, and click the Add button.

It is important to note that the name of this file needs to be consistent throughout your code. If you call it anything else (from what I have named it), you need to maintain that reference when adding the link to your generated CSS file.

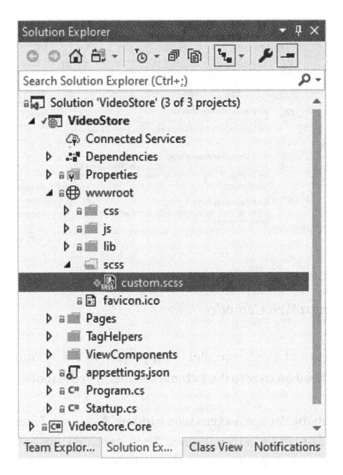

Figure 6-5. *Custom SCSS File Added*

Once you have added the file to your scss folder, your VideoStore project should look as in Figure 6-5. This is the file that we will add our SCSS syntax to. The CSS for our project will be compiled from this SCSS file.

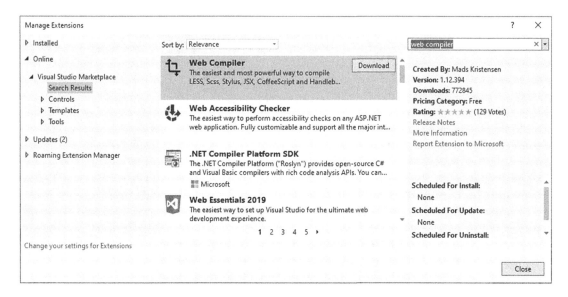

Figure 6-6. *Adding a Web Compiler*

The next task is to add a web compiler to the project. In Visual Studio 2019 version 16.6.2, you need to head on over to the Extensions menu in the toolbar and click Manage Extensions.

This will open up the Manage Extensions window. As seen in Figure 6-6, search for the term web compiler, and sort by relevance. The extension I am looking for here is created by Mads Kristensen. It is free and very easy to use.

Visual Studio might need to be closed and restarted to initiate the installation of this extension.

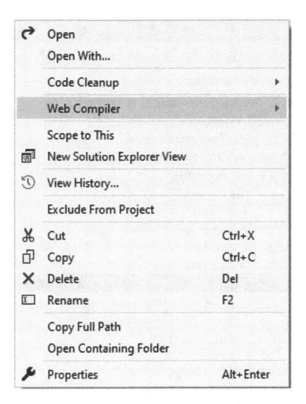

Figure 6-7. *Compiling the File*

Right-click the `custom.scss` file (Figure 6-7), and select Web Compiler ➤ Compile file.

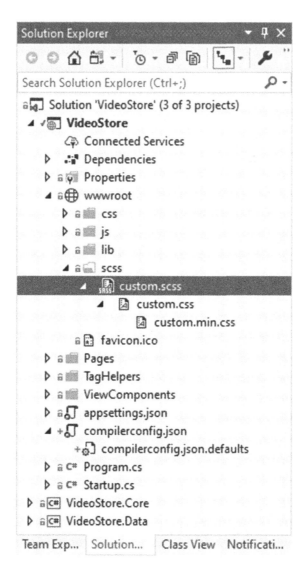

Figure 6-8. *The Compiled Files and Compiler Configuration*

You will now see that the `custom.scss` file generates a `custom.css` and a `custom.min.css` file nested underneath one another (Figure 6-8).

Also very important to note is the addition of a new file called `compilerconfig.json` (just below the `appsettings.json` file in Figure 6-8). It is this configuration file that will be used to control exactly where our generated CSS files are created.

Looking at the `compilerconfig.json` file in Listing 6-3, we can see that it defines the location of the generated CSS files in the same place as the `custom.scss` file.

Listing 6-3. The compilerconfig.json File

```
[
  {
    "outputFile": "wwwroot/scss/custom.css",
    "inputFile": "wwwroot/scss/custom.scss"
  }
]
```

I do not want the generated CSS file to live in my scss folder. There is already a folder for my CSS files in the wwwroot of my project. Go ahead and modify the output path for the generated CSS file to be the css folder as illustrated in Listing 6-4.

Listing 6-4. The Modified compilerconfig.json File

```
[
  {
    "outputFile": "wwwroot/css/custom.css",
    "inputFile": "wwwroot/scss/custom.scss"
  }
]
```

Whenever we save any changes to the scss file, the css file will be regenerated and placed in the css folder of the wwwroot. You can see these files created in the css folder in Figure 6-9.

To illustrate the power of SCSS, consider the Video Detail page. Remember that we created a video stats section that displays a short blurb about the particular video, a star rating, and a button to view the video page online. The stars used for the star rating were Font Awesome icons. The markup for this section was contained in the _VideoStats. cshtml partial view. The code is included again in Listing 6-5.

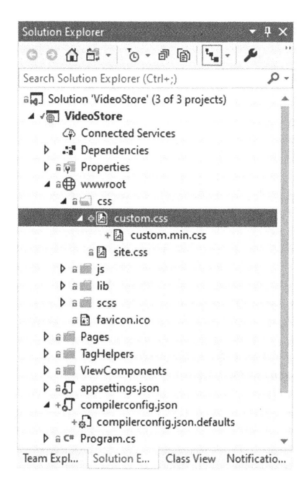

Figure 6-9. *The Relocated Compiled Files*

The stars were added by including the markup <i class="fas fa-star"></i> on each iteration of the rating received for the video. In other words, a rating of 4 will equal 4 stars.

Listing 6-5. The _VideoStats Partial View

```
@using VideoStore.Core
@model Video

<div class="card" style="width: 18rem;">
    <div class="card-header">
        @if (Model.Rating > 0)
        {
```

```
        for (int i = 0; i <= Model.Rating - 1; i++)
        {
            <i class="fas fa-star"></i>
        }
    }
    else
    {
        <h6>This video has not received any ratings yet</h6>
    }
    </div>
    <div class="card-body">
        <h5 class="card-title">@Model.Title</h5>
        <p class="card-text">@Model.Review</p>
        <a href="@Model.OnlineURL" class="btn btn-primary">View Online</a>
    </div>
</div>
```

Currently, the stars are black. I would like these stars to be a golden color. I am therefore going to be using CSS to change the color of the stars from black to golden. Open up the custom.scss file, and add the following code as illustrated in Listing 6-6.

Listing 6-6. Changing the Star Rating Color in the SCSS File

```
$star-color: #DAA520;


i.fas.fa-star {
    color: $star-color;
}
```

The scss file uses a variable called $star-color and sets it to the required hash code. All you need to do now is save your custom.scss file, and the custom.css file will be automatically updated with the changes. Looking at the generated CSS file, you will see the code in Listing 6-7.

Listing 6-7. The Generated CSS

```
i.fas.fa-star {
  color: #DAA520; }
```

This means that I only have to specify the color once and set a variable that I can use throughout my style sheet. If the color ever changes, I only need to change it in a single place. But we are not finished yet. We still need to add a reference to the generated CSS file on our layout page.

You will remember that we used a different layout page for the Video Detail page. This layout page was called _LayoutSpecial.cshtml. Open this file, and change the code in the <head> tag as illustrated in Listing 6-8.

Listing 6-8. Referencing the custom.css File

```
<head>
    <meta charset="utf-8" />
    <meta name="viewport" content="width=device-width, initial-scale=1.0" />
    <title>@ViewData["Title"] - VideoStore</title>
    <link rel="stylesheet" href="~/lib/bootstrap/dist/css/bootstrap.min.
    css" />
    <link rel="stylesheet" href="~/css/site.css" />

    <environment include="Development">
        <link rel="stylesheet" href="~/css/custom.css" />
    </environment>
    <environment exclude="Development">
        <link rel="stylesheet" href="~/css/custom.min.css" />
    </environment>
</head>
```

Here, you can see that we are telling ASP.NET Core to use the minified CSS file in production. When you run your Video Store application, and head on over to the Video Detail page, you will see that the stars are colored golden.

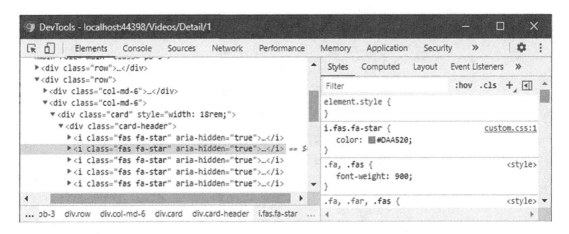

Figure 6-10. *The Applied CSS Style*

Looking at the applied styles in DevTools (Figure 6-10), you will see that the color style we specified is visible in the Styles tab.

SCSS Partial Files

Let's pause here to focus a bit on SCSS. Remember how I mentioned earlier that we can use partials? Well, partials are a way to modularize your code. Partial files are named with a leading underscore. This tells the web compiler not to compile this file into a CSS file of their own (like the custom.css file). Instead, these partial files can be used and imported or injected into other files and used there. To illustrate this, add a new SCSS file called _variables.scss to the scss folder as seen in Figure 6-11.

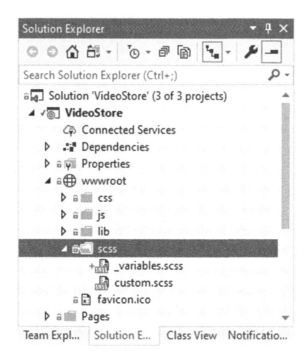

Figure 6-11. *Adding a _variables Partial File*

Inside the _variables partial file, add the code illustrated in Listing 6-9.

Listing 6-9. The _variables Partial File

```
/* Site Palette*/

$star-color: #DAA520;
```

We now have a separate place to store and change our variables used in the style sheets. Next, we need to modify the custom.scss file to import the _variables partial file as illustrated in Listing 6-10.

Listing 6-10. Importing the _variables Partial File

```
@import "_variables.scss";

i.fas.fa-star {
    color: $star-color;
}
```

We can now import the required partial files wherever we require them. We can also have more than one partial file, as long as the file name begins with a leading underscore.

We have made a few changes to the way we create our SCSS. We have split the functionality of variables into a separate partial file and can now control where we use that partial file. But have a look at the generated CSS file. It hasn't changed a bit. It has stayed the same. SCSS, therefore, allows us to structure the code used to style our application easily while producing the same output as expected.

Using SCSS @mixin

You can create mixins using the @mixin keyword. This allows you to create common sets of properties that can use default values for parameters but can still be overridden. We have used a partial file for variables, so let's use a partial file for our mixins.

Figure 6-12. *Partial File for Mixins*

Add a new partial file called `_mixins.scss` in the `scss` folder as seen in Figure 6-12. Add the code in Listing 6-11 to the file.

Listing 6-11. The Mixin File's Code

```scss
@mixin header-font($family: 'Times New Roman', $weight: 400, $style:
normal, $color: black) {
    font-family: $family, Helvetica, sans-serif;
    font-style: $style;
    font-weight: $weight;
    color: $color;
}
```

This mixin creates a header font that will use Times New Roman with a weight of 400, a normal style, and a color of black. In the custom.scss file, include the mixin file using @import, and apply the header font to H1 and H2 elements (Listing 6-12).

Listing 6-12. Import and Apply the Mixin

```scss
@import "_variables.scss";
@import "_mixins.scss";

i.fas.fa-star {
    color: $star-color;
}

h1 {
    @include header-font;
}

h2 {
    @include header-font('Arial', 200, normal, red);
}
```

You can see that the default values will be used when applied to H1 elements, but that we are overriding the values when we apply the style to H2 elements. Now modify the Index.cshtml page markup as illustrated in Listing 6-13.

Listing 6-13. Modified Index Page

```
@page
@model IndexModel
@{
    ViewData["Title"] = "Home page";
}

<div class="text-center">
    <h1 class="display-4">Welcome</h1>
    <p>Learn about <a href="https://docs.microsoft.com/aspnet/
    core">building Web apps with ASP.NET Core</a>.</p>
    <h2>In This Course</h2>
    <p>Add some course details here.</p>
</div>
```

Run your application and see the mixin applied to the header elements on the Index page (Figure 6-13).

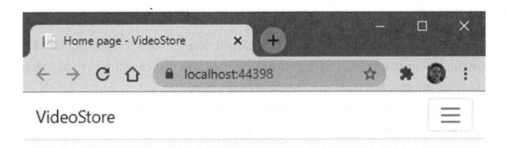

Figure 6-13. *The Index Page*

Another interesting thing to look at is the `custom.css` file illustrated in Listing 6-14. Our SCSS file contains minimal code, but using the power of partial files and `@import`, we can easily provide logic to style our markup.

Listing 6-14. The Compiled CSS

```
i.fas.fa-star {
  color: #DAA520; }

h1 {
  font-family: "Times New Roman", Helvetica, sans-serif;
  font-style: normal;
  font-weight: 400;
  color: black; }

h2 {
  font-family: "Arial", Helvetica, sans-serif;
  font-style: normal;
  font-weight: 200;
  color: red; }
```

While I would probably never use Times New Roman in an application, this does illustrate the power of mixins. I'm not sure if the medium you're using to read this book contains color images, but trust me, the H2 element is red.

Using mixins allows you to be very flexible when applying styles. You can just set it to the mixin name or tweak it slightly to suit your needs.

Using SCSS @extend

In SCSS, the @extend keyword will make developers think of Inheritance. This allows you to inherit the properties of one class and apply them to another. This is a great way to avoid code duplication.

To see how this works, start by creating a variable in the `_variables.scss` file called `$border-color` and make it red. Add another variable called `$highlight-color` and make it blue. The code can be seen in Listing 6-15.

Listing 6-15. Additional SCSS Variables

```scss
$star-color: #DAA520;

$border-color: #FF0000;
$highlight-color: #FF0000;
$highlight-text-color: #ffffff;
```

Because our custom.scss file imports the variables, we can reference those variables there. Consider the complete code for the custom.scss file in Listing 6-16.

Listing 6-16. Extending a Class in SCSS

```scss
@import "_variables.scss";
@import "_mixins.scss";

i.fas.fa-star {
    color: $star-color;
}

h1 {
    @include header-font;
}

h2 {
    @include header-font('Arial', 200, normal, red);
}

.pBorder {
    border: 2px solid $border-color;
}

.pBorder-highlight {
    @extend .pBorder;
    background-color: $highlight-color;
    color: $highlight-text-color;
}
```

I have added a style for a class called .pBorder. All this does is create a red border around the element applying that class. This is because it makes use of the $border-color variable.

Suppose I wanted to create a slight variation of this class but didn't want to add in the code from .pBorder a second time, I could use the @extend keyword as seen in Listing 6-16 for .pBorder-highlight. The line of code @extend .pBorder takes everything in .pBorder and applies it to .pBorder-highlight. Whatever else I define in .pBorder-highlight is only applied to .pBorder-highlight.

While the code in .pBorder is rather simple, imagine for a moment a class that applies a lot of styles. Extending classes now becomes worth its weight in gold, because it negates code duplication and allows you to keep any future changes to a single place.

Save your custom.scss file, and let's have a look at what the compiled CSS file looks like. You can see this in Listing 6-17.

Listing 6-17. The Compiled CSS File

```
i.fas.fa-star {
  color: #DAA520; }

h1 {
  font-family: "Times New Roman", Helvetica, sans-serif;
  font-style: normal;
  font-weight: 400;
  color: black; }

h2 {
  font-family: "Arial", Helvetica, sans-serif;
  font-style: normal;
  font-weight: 200;
  color: red; }

.pBorder, .pBorder-highlight {
  border: 2px solid #FF0000; }

.pBorder-highlight {
  background-color: #0000FF;
  color: #ffffff; }
```

If you compare the compiled CSS to the extended code in the SCSS file, then you can see that the extended code in the SCSS file makes the intent clearer and more concise. Let's go ahead and apply these classes to the Index.cshtml page as illustrated in Listing 6-18.

Listing 6-18. Classes Applied to Index Page

```
@page
@model IndexModel
@{
    ViewData["Title"] = "Home page";
}

<div class="text-center">
    <h1 class="display-4">Welcome</h1>
    <p class="pBorder">Learn about <a href="https://docs.microsoft.com/
    aspnet/core">building Web apps with ASP.NET Core</a>.</p>
    <h2>In This Course</h2>
    <p class="pBorder-highlight">Add some course details here.</p>
</div>
```

If you run the application, you will see the styles applied to the <p> elements on the Index page in Figure 6-14.

Figure 6-14. *The Index Page Applying the pBorder Classes*

Being able to extend classes in SCSS allows you to be extremely flexible. Not having to rewrite code is also great, because should you need to change something further down the line, you only need to change it in a single place.

Using SCSS Functions

Using functions with SCSS is exactly what you think it is. What functions allow you to do is create some logic that can be applied wherever you import your partial file.

A partial file will be used to contain often used functions that can then be imported into the custom.scss file.

This makes using functions very powerful when creating styles with SCSS.

To see how this works, start by creating a new partial file called `_functions.scss` in the `scss` folder. This can be seen in Figure 6-15. This file will contain all the functions that we write and that must be applied in the style sheets.

Figure 6-15. *The Functions Partial File*

What I want to do is create a function that will calculate element padding for me based on a supplied value, multiplied by a base value. If no value is supplied, then a default value must be used. Before we can add this function, we need to add a variable $base-padding to the _variables.scss partial file.

Listing 6-19. The Base Padding Value

```
/* Site Palette*/

$star-color: #DAA520;

$border-color: #FF0000;
$highlight-color: #0000FF;
$highlight-text-color: #ffffff;

/* Base Padding */

$base-padding: 2px;
```

As seen in Listing 6-19, the base padding value is 2 pixels. Next, in the _functions. scss file, add the code in Listing 6-20.

Listing 6-20. The Padding Calculation Function

```scss
@import "_variables.scss";

@function padding-calc($factor: 1) {
    @return $base-padding * $factor;
}
```

Because we are using the $base-padding variable, we need to import the _variables.scss partial file. Functions are created using the @function keyword followed by the function name. Parameters can be passed to the function. In the example in Listing 6-20, the function takes a parameter called $factor. If no value is supplied, then the default value of 1 will be applied to the $factor. The function then returns the result of multiplying the base padding with the factor to determine the element padding.

To see this in action, modify your custom.scss file by importing the _functions. scss file and applying the function to an element to calculate the padding. This is illustrated in Listing 6-21. You will see that the padding-calc function has been applied to the .pBorder class.

Listing 6-21. Using the Function

```scss
@import "_variables.scss";
@import "_mixins.scss";
@import "_functions.scss";

i.fas.fa-star {
    color: $star-color;
}

h1 {
    @include header-font;
}

h2 {
    @include header-font('Arial', 200, normal, red);
}
```

```
.pBorder {
    border: 2px solid $border-color;
    padding: padding-calc(5);
}

.pBorder-highlight {
    @extend .pBorder;
    background-color: $highlight-color;
    color: $highlight-text-color;
}
```

Save the custom.scss file, and inspect the generated custom.css file. You can see the resulting code in Listing 6-22. In this instance, because we supplied a value of 5 to the padding-calc function, the resulting value for padding was calculated as 10.

Listing 6-22. The .pBorder Class in the Generated CSS

```
.pBorder, .pBorder-highlight {
  border: 2px solid #FF0000;
  padding: 10px; }
```

Change the custom.scss file, and remove the value of 5 passed to the padding-calc function (Listing 6-23).

Listing 6-23. The padding-calc Without a Parameter

```
.pBorder {
    border: 2px solid $border-color;
    padding: padding-calc();
}
```

If you save the custom.scss file and inspect the generated custom.css file, you will notice that the calculated value for the padding in the .pBorder class has changed to 2 pixels (Listing 6-24).

Listing 6-24. The Default Parameter Value Applied

```
.pBorder, .pBorder-highlight {
  border: 2px solid #FF0000;
  padding: 2px; }
```

This is because the default parameter value of 1 for the `$factor` was applied to the calculation with the `$base-padding` value of 2.

Working with Chrome Developer Tools

The web application in this book is run in Google Chrome. It is for that reason that I have included a section on Chrome Developer Tools in this chapter. Developer tools are also available in other browsers, so if you use a different browser for debugging, the features and functionality explained in this section might differ from yours.

Debugging your web application isn't always a case of placing a breakpoint in the C# code and stepping through the code. Sometimes, you need a way to inspect and step through client-side code such as jQuery, or to modify CSS. This is where Chrome Developer Tools can come in handy.

Running your web application, you should see the `Index` page that we modified earlier in the previous section on SCSS. Right-click the page (or right-click an element on the page such as a heading), and click `Inspect` from the context menu. You can also hold down `Ctrl+Shift+I` to open the developer tools.

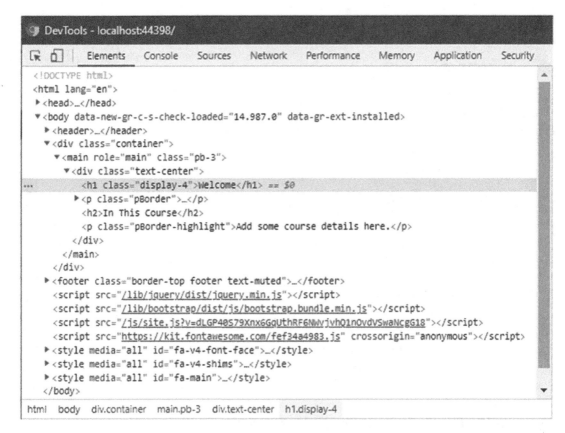

Figure 6-16. *The Page Markup Displayed in DevTools*

Expanding the elements, you should see the header elements as illustrated in Figure 6-16.

If you right-clicked the Welcome heading, you will be taken directly to the H1 element.

This is the markup for the Index page, and you can modify the layout directly in DevTools.

Dragging Elements

The elements displayed in DevTools are all draggable. With the H1 element selected, click and drag it to below the H2 element.

Figure 6-17. *The H1 Element Dragged to Below the H2 Element*

Your markup will look as illustrated in Figure 6-17. Notice how when you drag the elements around, the web page is updated to display the changed layout (Figure 6-18).

Figure 6-18. *The Updated Web Page*

You are now in a position to see how the page will look by dragging elements around the page. This is great for changing the layout of a page without having to make permanent changes to your code. When you refresh the page, the layout of the elements is reset to what they were before you started moving them around.

Adding and Modifying Styles

It is also possible to modify the CSS in DevTools. This is a fantastic way to check if the styling changes look nice or if planned changes will have the intended effect.

With the page reset by refreshing the page, right-click the H2 element and click Inspect. Note that you don't need to close DevTools to inspect an element. You can inspect an element while DevTools is open. The focused element in DevTools will jump to the H2 element as seen in Figure 6-19.

Figure 6-19. *The Highlighted H2 Element*

You can see that the CSS for the page is displayed in the Styles tab on the right. Thinking back to the code we added to the SCSS file for the H2 element, you will remember that we included the @mixin as seen in Listing 6-25.

Listing 6-25. The SCSS Code for the H2 Element

```
h2 {
    @include header-font('Arial', 200, normal, red);
}
```

The generated CSS specifies that the font color must be red. In the Styles tab, we can change this color by clicking the little red block next to the color attribute (Figure 6-20).

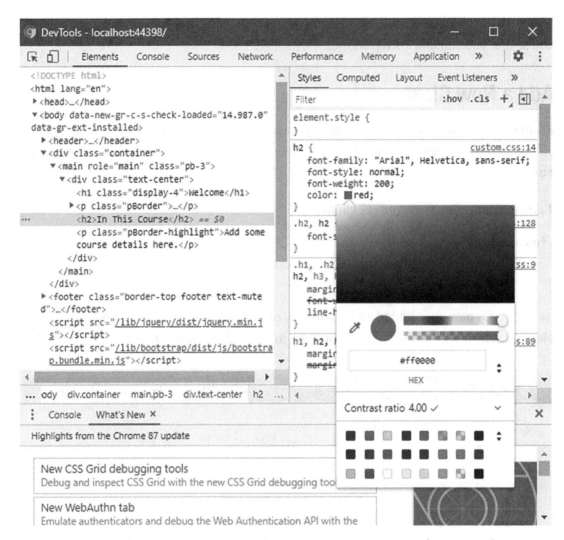

***Figure 6-20.** Changing the Font Color of the H2 Element*

The color palette that opens up allows you to change the color. Notice how the web page is immediately updated as you change the color. The Styles tab allows you to do much more than just changing styles. You can add new styles, classes, and toggle state by clicking the icons to the right of the Filter illustrated in Figure 6-21.

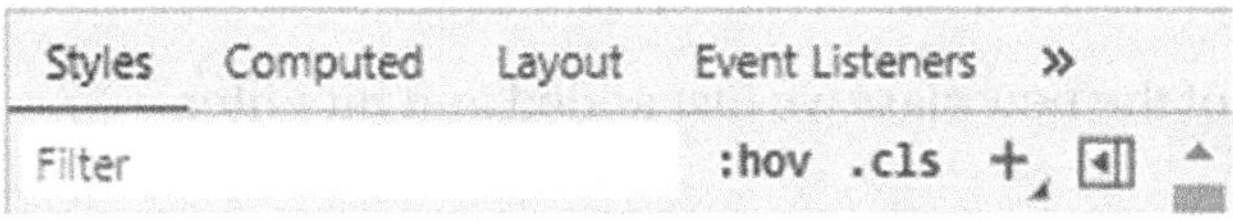

***Figure 6-21.** Adding Styles, Classes, and State*

With the H2 element selected, click the plus (+) button. You will see that a style rule is added that you can add attributes to.

Add a New Class

Adding a new class to an element is just as easy. Close the browser and modify the custom.scss file by adding a new class called .featuredH2 that applies a different font size and color (Listing 6-26).

Listing 6-26. The featuredH2 Class

```
.featuredH2 {
    @include header-font('Arial', 300, normal, gold);
}
```

With this new class added and compiled, run the web application again. With the H2 element selected, click the .cls button seen in Figure 6-21 as illustrated in Figure 6-22.

Figure 6-22. *Adding a New Class*

Type the name of the new class we just added and hit Enter.

It is important to note that all these changes are just temporary. When you refresh or close your page, all the changes you made will be lost.

You will see that the web page is updated as the new class style is applied to the H2 element. The H2 element is also updated to show the added class as seen in Figure 6-23.

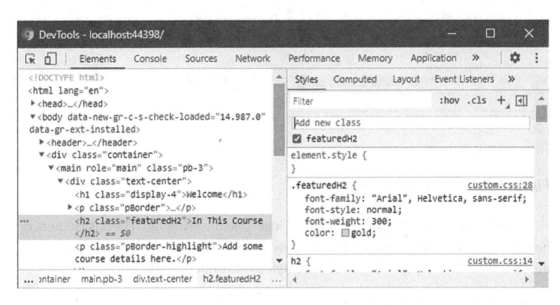

Figure 6-23. *The New featuredH2 Class Applied*

This allows you to test different classes on elements on your web page without having to change any code.

Testing State Changes

If you happen to have elements that respond to state changes, you can trigger the state of an element using DevTools. As it turns out, there is a link on the Index page. The link is just below the H1 element. Right-click the link, and click Inspect. As seen in Figure 6-21, click the :hov button, and check the :hover state as seen in Figure 6-24.

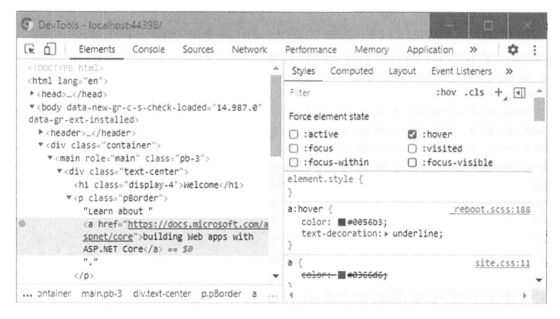

Figure 6-24. *The Hover State Triggered*

You will see that the a:hover style rule is loaded in the Styles tab. The link element is now in a permanent hover state while the :hover state is checked. You can now modify the element state. Change the :hover state style as illustrated in Listing 6-27.

Listing 6-27. The Modified Hover State

```
a:hover {
    color: #dc3545;
    text-decoration: line-through;
}
```

When you have done this, uncheck the :hover state, and move your mouse over the link on the web page. You will see that the changes you made to the hover state of the link are now applied whenever you hover your mouse over the link.

Forcing the state of an element allows you to ensure that the style you want is visually applied to allow you to modify the style easily.

Throttling Network Speed

Sometimes you need to understand how your site will perform when users access it from a slow Internet connection. To test this, open DevTools, and click the Network tab as seen in Figure 6-25.

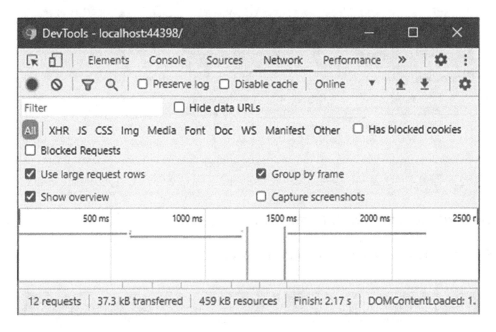

Figure 6-25. *Viewing the Network Tab*

Here, you will see on the second toolbar that the site shows Online. Next to the text Online, you will see a down arrow. Click this down arrow to reveal the different presets available as seen in Figure 6-26.

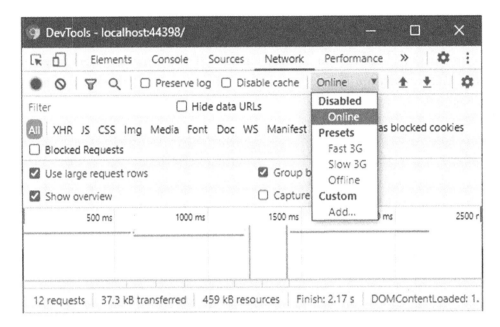

Figure 6-26. *Selecting the Throttling State*

Selecting Slow 3G will throttle your site speed.

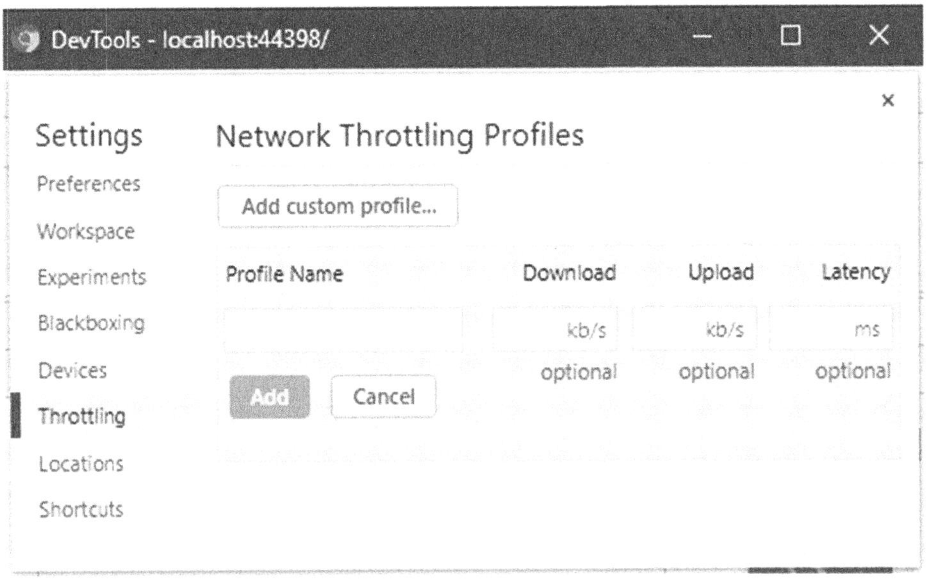

Figure 6-27. *Adding a Custom Profile*

Being able to throttle your network speed allows you to test the performance of your code on the page. You can even add a custom Network Throttling Profile as seen in Figure 6-27. This is extremely useful when you have a specific networking requirement that your site needs to adhere to.

Wrapping Up

The DevTools in Chrome allows you to do a lot more than what I have shown in this chapter. I could write a separate book on using the developer tools in Chrome. Unfortunately, I only have a few pages to do this in, and I simply wanted to introduce some key concepts here in this chapter. In addition to what I have shown here, Chrome Developer Tools allows you to do the following:

- Add breakpoints to scripts allowing you to debug them.

- Step through the script execution while in a breakpoint state.

- Add Event Listener breakpoints on scripts for events such as click and mouseover events.

- Add variables to a Watch as well as add expressions to the Watch.

- Log information to the Console window in DevTools.

- Save your Console output.

- Audit the website's speed.

- Simulate different mobile devices to test how your site is displayed.

Google has a rich set of online documentation available for Chrome DevTools at the following link: `https://developers.google.com/web/tools/chrome-devtools/`.

There is a lot to learn there, and the more you familiarize yourself with it, the more benefit it will provide you when debugging your web applications.

CHAPTER 7

Exploring Middleware

In this chapter, we will be taking a closer look at middleware and the role it plays in ASP. NET Core. Understanding the role of middleware will help you structure your ASP.NET Core applications to make efficient use of middleware and the requests they handle.

What Is Middleware

Let's first answer the most glaring question. What exactly is middleware? The simple answer is the following: Middleware can be thought of as a pipeline of code that handles requests and responses. Middleware chooses to pass requests to the next bit of code in the pipeline or doing something with that request before passing it on.

Request delegates are used to build this pipeline of software that handles each HTTP request. The request delegates are configured by using the Run, Map, and Use extension methods. Each request delegate can be specified in-line (in-line middleware) or as a reusable class.

Looking at the Startup.cs class in our application, the Configure method (Listing 7-1) is what ASP.NET Core uses to work out what middleware needs to be executed.

Listing 7-1. The Configure Method

```
public void Configure(IApplicationBuilder app, IWebHostEnvironment env)
{
    if (env.IsDevelopment())
    {
        _ = app.UseDeveloperExceptionPage();
    }
```

© Dirk Strauss 2021
D. Strauss, *Creating ASP.NET Core Web Applications*, https://doi.org/10.1007/978-1-4842-6828-5_7

```
else
{
    _ = app.UseExceptionHandler("/Error");
    _ = app.UseHsts();
}

_ = app.UseHttpsRedirection();
_ = app.UseStaticFiles();

_ = app.UseRouting();
_ = app.UseAuthorization();
_ = app.UseSession();
_ = app.UseEndpoints(endpoints =>
  {
      _ = endpoints.MapRazorPages();
  });
}
```

Middleware is installed by calling extension methods on an object implementing the IApplicationBuilder Interface. This Interface provides the mechanisms to configure the application's request pipeline. Looking at the code in Listing 7-1, you can see that we have added the UseDeveloperExceptionPage middleware only when in development mode. If we're not in development mode, we use the UseExceptionHandler and UseHsts middleware. Other middleware installed in our Configure method is middleware such as UseRouting and UseAuthorization and so on.

By doing this, we are building up a request pipeline (Figure 7-1). When an HTTP request comes into this pipeline, the first piece of middleware will look at the request and perform some function (the function of work it was designed to perform). If this request looks good, it will be passed on to the next piece of middleware in our pipeline. This process repeats itself, but if one piece of middleware decides that the request is not valid, this request pipeline can be short-circuited. Middleware that short-circuits the request pipeline is called terminal middleware because it prevents the subsequent middleware components from being able to process the request.

Figure 7-1. *The Middleware Pipeline*

An example of this might be where authorization fails and that authorization middleware returns a failed response. It will not pass the request further down the line and therefore terminates that request because of the authorization failure.

As you can see from Figure 7-1, the middleware pipeline receives requests and sends out responses. This means it is bidirectional and that for each request that happens, some kind of response will occur. That response could be an error, or a page, or some JSON. Middleware is, therefore, very important in ASP.NET Core because it defines the behavior of your application. Let's have a look at some of the installed middleware in our application.

Handling Exceptions

Because of the bidirectionality of the middleware request pipeline, any middleware at the beginning of the pipeline is there because it needs to be the first piece of code to do something with an incoming request or the last piece of code to do something with an outgoing response. In Listing 7-1, our `Configure` method installs the `UseDeveloperExceptionPage` when in development mode, first. It just passes the requests it receives on to the next piece of middleware, but if any of those pieces of middleware throws an exception, the `UseDeveloperExceptionPage` then cares about the response and will display a developer exception. It is first in the request pipeline because it needs to be last in the response.

When we are in production, a more friendly error page is displayed to the user, without the stack trace, for example, that we would see when using the developer exception page.

UseHsts

We also tell the application to HSTS (HTTP Strict Transport Security Protocol) in the response header. The UseHsts extension method was implemented from ASP.NET Core 2.1 and later. When a browser that supports HSTS receives this header, it will force all communication over HTTPS. It also prevents users from using untrusted or invalid certificates and will not allow the user to temporarily trust such a certificate.

HSTS is enforced by the client and, therefore, is slightly limited in that the client must support HSTS. It also requires at least one successful HTTPS request to establish the HSTS policy.

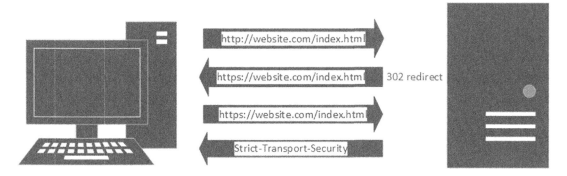

Figure 7-2. *The HSTS Response*

This can be seen in Figure 7-2. Once the secure request is made to the server, a header is sent back called Strict Transport Security. This tells the client that for a specific duration (default is 30 days), every request to this site must use HTTPS.

If the user comes back to the site within that duration, regardless of whether they clicked a link, typed a URL, or used a bookmark, the browser will make the initial request over HTTPS (Figure 7-3).

Figure 7-3. *Subsequent Requests Within HSTS Duration*

Don't use HSTS in development, because these settings are highly cacheable by browsers. This is why the UseHsts middleware is installed when we're only in production.

Furthermore, you can configure options for HSTS in the ConfigureServices method as seen in Listing 7-2.

Listing 7-2. HSTS Options in ConfigureServices

```
_ = services.AddHsts(opts =>
{
    opts.Preload = true;
    opts.IncludeSubDomains = true;
    opts.MaxAge = TimeSpan.FromDays(60);
    opts.ExcludedHosts.Add("www.somesite.com");
});
```

Here, you will see the following options:

- Preload

- IncludeSubDomains

- MaxAge

- ExcludedHosts

The Preload option tells the browser to use HTTPS before it comes to our site. This means that the initial HSTS response isn't necessary as seen in Figure 7-2. The first time the browser comes to our site, it will use HTTPS right from the get-go. You can find more info on https://hstspreload.org.

229

The IncludeSubDomains option is self-explanatory, but it tells the browser to apply the HSTS policy to any subdomains for the host.

You can also set the MaxAge which tells the browser how long we want the browser to keep track of the fact that we want to use HSTS.

Lastly, we can exclude any hosts by adding the ExcludedHosts option.

UseHttpsRedirection

The UseHttpsRedirection middleware will send an HTTP Redirect instruction to any browser trying to access the site via HTTP.

UseStaticFiles

As the name suggests, this enables static files to be served. Static files are files such as HTML, CSS, images, and JavaScript. The default directory for static files is the wwwroot directory. The UseStaticFiles middleware will therefore look for a folder called wwwroot by default. If we don't want to call the web root wwwroot, then we need to tell ASP.NET Core where the static files can be served from. We can do this by using the UseWebRoot method on the web builder in the Program.cs file as seen in Listing 7-3.

Listing 7-3. Changing the Web Root Folder

```
public static IHostBuilder CreateHostBuilder(string[] args) =>
    Host.CreateDefaultBuilder(args)
        .ConfigureWebHostDefaults(webBuilder =>
        {
            webBuilder.UseStartup<Startup>();
            webBuilder.UseWebRoot("wwwsite");
        });
```

Here, we are telling ASP.NET Core that the web root of the application has changed to wwwsite. This is, however, not something I want to do, so I'll leave my web root as wwwroot.

This means that static files are accessible via a relative path to the wwwroot directory. If you expand the wwwroot folder, you will see css, js, and lib by default. Because the UseStaticFiles middleware marks files in the wwwroot as servable, referencing a CSS file as follows "~/css/custom.css" tells ASP.NET Core to look in the web root for the file by using the tilde ~ character.

If you need to keep your static files outside of the wwwroot folder (in a StaticFiles folder, e.g., as illustrated in Figure 7-4), you can configure the StaticFileOptions of the UseStaticFiles middleware as seen in Listing 7-4.

Note that you will need to import the namespaces Microsoft.Extensions. FileProviders and System.IO.

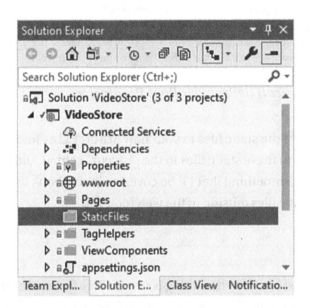

Figure 7-4. *Using a StaticFiles Folder Outside wwwroot*

This means that you can now reference a CSS file in the css folder under the StaticFiles folder as "~/StaticFiles/css/custom.css".

Listing 7-4. Use Static Files Outside of wwwroot

```
_ = app.UseStaticFiles(new StaticFileOptions
{
    FileProvider = new PhysicalFileProvider(Path.Combine(env.
    ContentRootPath, "StaticFiles")), RequestPath = "/StaticFiles"
});
```

It is interesting to note that the parameter of the `PhysicalFileProvider` is called `root` as seen in Figure 7-5.

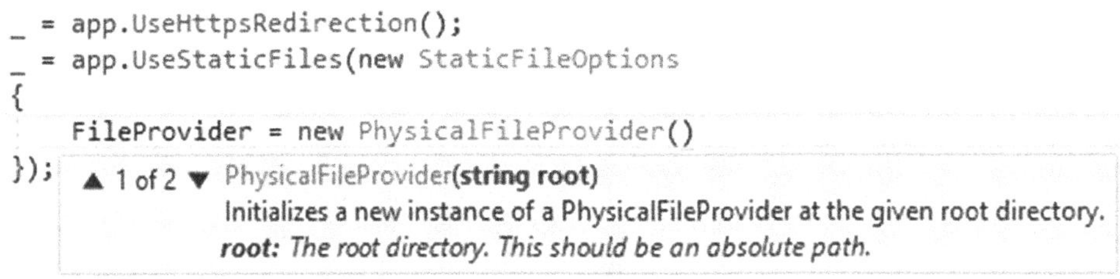

Figure 7-5. *The PhysicalFileProvider Root Parameter*

If you want to move the static files to your new `StaticFiles` folder, you will have to update the references to these static files in the `_Layout.cshtml` and `_LayoutSpecial.cshtml` file. This is not something that I'll be covering in this book though. Just know that if you had to move static files outside of the web root, you can.

UseRouting

When an HTTP request is received, routing is responsible for matching and dispatching the requests to the endpoints. This means that `UseRouting` adds route matching to the pipeline. The middleware then finds the best matching endpoint based on the incoming request.

UseSession

If you have been working with ASP.NET applications for any length of time, you will know that sessions allow us to store user data. To use sessions in our web application, we need to call the `AddSession` method in the `ConfigureServices` method and add the `UseSession` middleware in the `Configure` method.

UseEndpoints with MapRazorPages

This adds endpoint execution to the pipeline that will run a delegate associated with the matched endpoint. When used, this middleware will add Razor page endpoints to the pipeline.

Creating Custom Middleware

Previously in this chapter, you saw that ASP.NET Core includes a rich set of built-in middleware components. By now, you would also have noticed that the order in which middleware appears in your pipeline matters. While there are a lot of middleware components to choose from, sometimes, you might need to create a custom middleware component. Adding custom middleware components isn't all that difficult. As it turns out, Visual Studio includes a template for creating a standard middleware class. Create a new folder called CustomMiddleware in your project root, right-click it, and add a new item. The Add New Item window is displayed as seen in Figure 7-6.

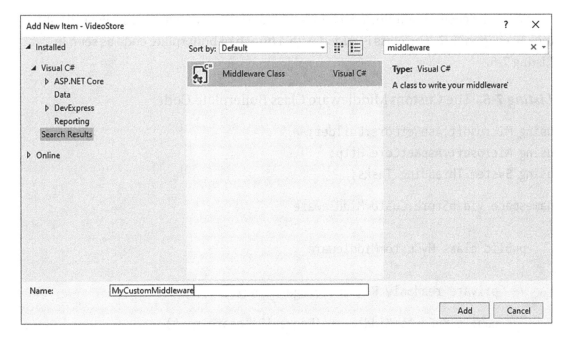

Figure 7-6. The Middleware Template

In the search text box, type in the word middleware, and find the C# middleware class template. I just called the custom middleware class MyCustomMiddleware.

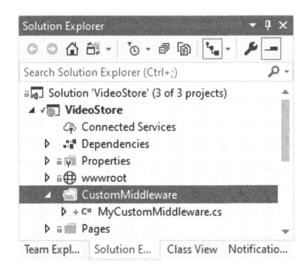

Figure 7-7. *Custom Middleware Class Added*

When the custom middleware class is added to your project, your project should look like Figure 7-7. The class is added with a bunch of boilerplate code as seen in Listing 7-5.

Listing 7-5. The Custom Middleware Class Boilerplate Code

```
using Microsoft.AspNetCore.Builder;
using Microsoft.AspNetCore.Http;
using System.Threading.Tasks;

namespace VideoStore.CustomMiddleware
{
    public class MyCustomMiddleware
    {
        private readonly RequestDelegate _next;

        public MyCustomMiddleware(RequestDelegate next)
        {
            _next = next;
        }
```

```
    public Task Invoke(HttpContext httpContext)
    {
        return _next(httpContext);
    }
}

public static class MyCustomMiddlewareExtensions
{
    public static IApplicationBuilder UseMyCustomMiddleware(this
    IApplicationBuilder builder)
    {
        return builder.UseMiddleware<MyCustomMiddleware>();
    }

}
}
```

From the code in Listing 7-5, you will see that the Invoke method calls the next delegate/middleware in the pipeline. That is all it does. This is where you want to add your custom code.

Secondly, you will notice the static class MyCustomMiddlewareExtensions that contains an extension method called UseMyCustomMiddleware. This extension method exposes the custom middleware through IApplicationBuilder so that it can be added to the request pipeline. All that I want to do in my custom middleware is write out a log entry. Start by modifying the MyCustomMiddleware class as illustrated in Listing 7-6.

Listing 7-6. Modified Custom Middleware Class

```
using Microsoft.AspNetCore.Builder;
using Microsoft.AspNetCore.Http;
using Microsoft.Extensions.Logging;
using System.Threading.Tasks;

namespace VideoStore.CustomMiddleware
{
    public class MyCustomMiddleware
    {
        private readonly RequestDelegate _next;
        private readonly ILogger _logger;
```

235

```
    public MyCustomMiddleware(RequestDelegate next, ILoggerFactory
    loggerFactory)
    {
        _next = next;
        _logger = loggerFactory.CreateLogger("MiddlewareLogger");
    }

    public async Task InvokeAsync(HttpContext httpContext)
    {
        _logger.LogInformation("**** Middleware Invoke Called ****");
        await _next(httpContext);
    }
}

public static class MyCustomMiddlewareExtensions
{
    public static IApplicationBuilder UseMyCustomMiddleware(this
    IApplicationBuilder builder)
    {
        return builder.UseMiddleware<MyCustomMiddleware>();
    }
}
}
```

I have modified the Invoke method to be asynchronous (changing the method name to InvokeAsync as per convention). Secondly, I have added an ILoggerFactory via dependency injection to create a logger for me that I can use in my custom middleware. In the Invoke method, you would want to write your custom code before the call is made to _next. All I did was write a log message **** Middleware Invoke Called ****.

With this in place, open your Startup.cs class, and add the using statement for VideoStore.CustomMiddleware. You can now add the custom middleware before the UseHttpsRedirection middleware as seen in Listing 7-7.

Listing 7-7. The Modified Configure Method

```
public void Configure(IApplicationBuilder app, IWebHostEnvironment env)
{
    if (env.IsDevelopment())
    {
        _ = app.UseDeveloperExceptionPage();
    }
    else
    {
        _ = app.UseExceptionHandler("/Error");
        _ = app.UseHsts();
    }

    _ = app.UseMyCustomMiddleware();
    _ = app.UseHttpsRedirection();
    _ = app.UseStaticFiles();
    _ = app.UseRouting();
    _ = app.UseAuthorization();
    _ = app.UseSession();
    _ = app.UseEndpoints(endpoints =>
    {
        _ = endpoints.MapRazorPages();
    });
}
```

Build your application and run it. From the View menu in Visual Studio, select Output, or type Ctrl+Alt+O. The Output pane will be displayed. In the Show output from drop-down, select VideoStore - ASP.NET Core Web Server. You will see the output displayed as illustrated in Figure 7-8.

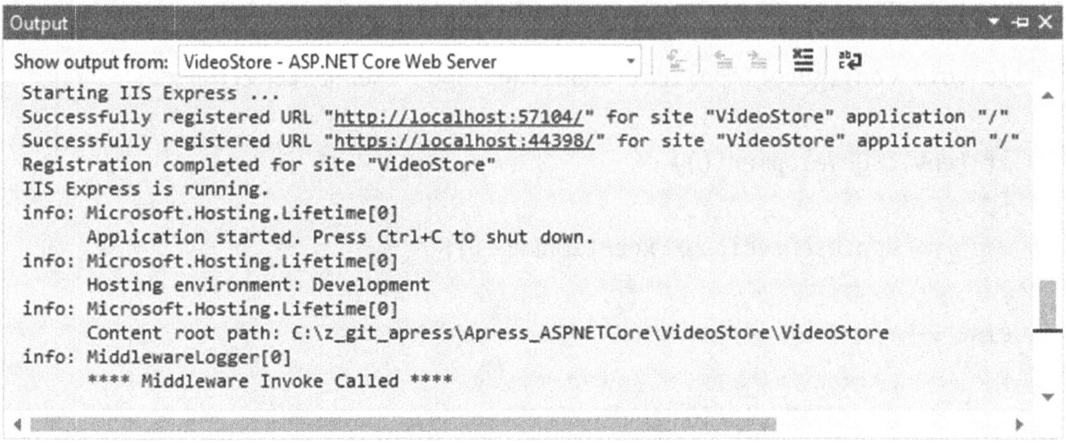

Figure 7-8. *The Output Window Showing Log Messages*

You will see the `MiddlewareLogger` displayed in the `Output` with the message ****
`Middleware Invoke Called` ****. Creating custom middleware components can give you a lot of flexibility when the built-in middleware just doesn't quite suit your needs.

Logging Information

Logging information is very useful when developing applications like ours. Sometimes, you might want to see why your custom middleware isn't working, and we already saw in the previous section how to add logging to a custom middleware component.

Let's have a look at how to add logging to our `VideoError` page. Open up the `VideoError.cshtml.cs` page, and modify the code as illustrated in Listing 7-8.

Listing 7-8. The Modified VideoErrorModel Class

```
using Microsoft.AspNetCore.Mvc;
using Microsoft.AspNetCore.Mvc.RazorPages;
using Microsoft.Extensions.Logging;

namespace VideoStore.Pages.Videos
{
    public class VideoErrorModel : PageModel
    {
        private readonly ILogger<VideoErrorModel> _logger;
```

```
[BindProperty(SupportsGet = true)]
public string Message { get; set; }

public VideoErrorModel(ILogger<VideoErrorModel> logger)
{
    _logger = logger;
}

public void OnGet()
{
    _logger.LogError(Message);
}
    }
}
```

All that I am doing here is adding an ILogger to the constructor via dependency injection and saving that off to a private field called _logger that I can use throughout my VideoErrorModel. All that I then do in the OnGet is log the error.

Run the application, and open up a Video Detail page. Your URL should be something like localhost:44398/Videos/Detail/3 where 44398 is my port number which will differ from yours, and 3 is the ID of the video we are viewing the detail for. Your video ID will probably also be different. Change the video ID to something impossible (force an error here by changing the video ID to an ID not in your database), and hit Enter.

Opening up the Output window from the View ➤ Output menu in Visual Studio or by holding down Ctrl+Alt+O, you will see the error logged in the output when you change the drop-down to VideoStore - ASP.NET Core Web Server (Figure 7-9).

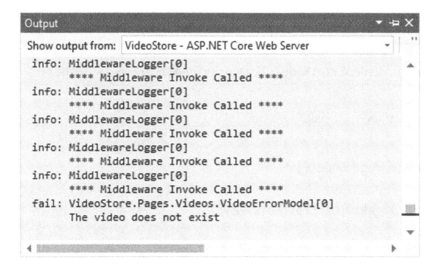

Figure 7-9. *The Error Output Logged*

While this example of logging isn't terrifically detailed, you can get an idea of how you could implement logging in various sections of your application.

Opening up the appsettings.json file, you will see that there is a Logging configuration section in this file (Listing 7-9).

Listing 7-9. The appsettings.json File

```
{
  "Logging": {
    "LogLevel": {
      "Default": "Information",
      "Microsoft": "Warning",
      "Microsoft.Hosting.Lifetime": "Information"
    }
  },
  "AllowedHosts": "*",
  "VideoListPageTitle": "Video Store - Videos List",
  "ConnectionStrings": {
    "VideoConn": "Data Source=(localdb)\\MSSQLLocalDB;Initial
    Catalog=VideoStore;Integrated Security=True;"
  }
}
```

If you expand the `appsettings.json` file in the Solution Explorer, you will see that there is an `appsettings.Development.json` file nested under it (Figure 7-10). Therefore, logging is provided by the `Logging` section of the `appsettings.{Environment}.json` file. Open the `appsettings.Development.json` file, and you will see the JSON as illustrated in Listing 7-10.

Listing 7-10. The appsettings.Development.json File

```
{
  "Logging": {
    "LogLevel": {
      "Default": "Information",
      "Microsoft": "Warning",
      "Microsoft.Hosting.Lifetime": "Information"
    }
  }
}
```

The keys in this `appsettings.Development.json` file will override the keys in the `appsettings.json` when we are in development. To add a JSON file for production, just add a new JSON file to your project, and call it `appsettings.Production.json`. It will automatically be nested under the `appsettings.json` file as seen in Figure 7-11.

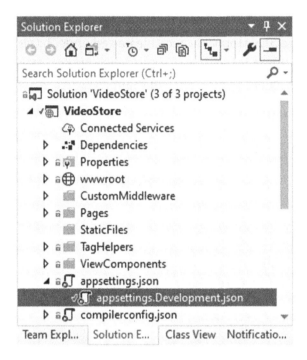

Figure 7-10. *The appsettings.Development.json File*

The environment version of the loaded appsettings file is based on the IHostingEnvironment.EnvironmentName.

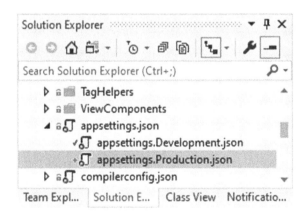

Figure 7-11. *The appsettings.Production.json File Added*

Looking back at Listing 7-10, you will see that the following categories are specified:

- Default

- Microsoft

- Microsoft.Hosting.Lifetime

The different categories log at different levels. The `Default` category, for example, logs at a log level of `Information`, while the `Microsoft` category logs at a level of `Warning` and higher. The `Microsoft.Hosting.Lifetime` category is very specific as opposed to the `Microsoft` category which is quite broad.

Because we have not specified a logging provider, the `LogLevel` will apply to all logging providers that are enabled.

Logging providers store logs from your application, except for the Console provider which displays logs.

The `CreateDefaultBuilder` method in the `Program.cs` file initializes a new instance of the `HostBuilder` class that adds the following logging providers:

- Console

- Debug

- EventSource

- EventLog (Windows only)

As with a lot of the defaults used by the creation of the HostBuilder class, you can override the logging providers as seen in Listing 7-11.

Listing 7-11. Override the Default Logging Providers

```
public static IHostBuilder CreateHostBuilder(string[] args) =>
    Host.CreateDefaultBuilder(args)
        .ConfigureLogging(log =>
        {
            log.ClearProviders();
            log.AddDebug();
        })
        .ConfigureWebHostDefaults(webBuilder =>
```

```
    {
        webBuilder.UseStartup<Startup>();
    });
```

First, we remove all instances of the ILoggerProvider by calling ClearProviders. Then, we add the Debug logging provider.

Only Logging What Is Necessary

The problem with log files is that, sometimes, developers can get a bit overeager. When I am in a development environment, it is probably a good idea to see informational logging, but in a production environment, I might only care about warnings and errors. Think back to the custom middleware we created in Listing 7-6. Let's modify the code slightly as illustrated in Listing 7-12.

Listing 7-12. Modified InvokeAsync Method in Custom Middleware

```
public class MyCustomMiddleware
{
    private readonly RequestDelegate _next;
    private readonly ILogger _logger;

    public MyCustomMiddleware(RequestDelegate next, ILoggerFactory
    loggerFactory)
    {
        _next = next;
        _logger = loggerFactory.CreateLogger("MiddlewareLogger");
    }

    public async Task InvokeAsync(HttpContext httpContext)
    {
        _logger.LogInformation("**** Info Middleware Invoke Called ****");
        _logger.LogWarning("**** Warning Middleware Invoke Called ****");
        _logger.LogError("**** Error Middleware Invoke Called ****");
        await _next(httpContext);
    }
}
```

I have added three log outputs, one each for `LogInformation`, `LogWarning`, and `LogError`. Next, look back at Listing 7-10, and notice how we have set the default log level in the `appsettings.Development.json` file to `Information`. Run the web application, and view the `Output` window. To open up the `Output` window, click the `View ➤ Output` menu in Visual Studio, or hold down `Ctrl+Alt+O`. You should see the following output as illustrated in Figure 7-12.

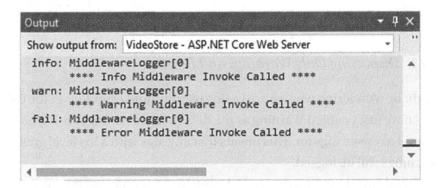

Figure 7-12. *The Output Window Displaying Middleware Log Output*

All three log outputs are displayed in the `Output` window. We can control exactly which log outputs we see by editing the appsettings.Development.json file as seen in Listing 7-13.

Listing 7-13. The Modified appsettings.Development.json File

```
{
  "Logging": {
    "LogLevel": {
      "Default": "Warning",
      "Microsoft": "Warning",
      "Microsoft.Hosting.Lifetime": "Information"
    }
  }
}
```

Change the default log level to Warning as seen in Listing 7-13, and run your application again. View the `Output` window, and notice that the Information logs are now excluded from being logged (Figure 7-13).

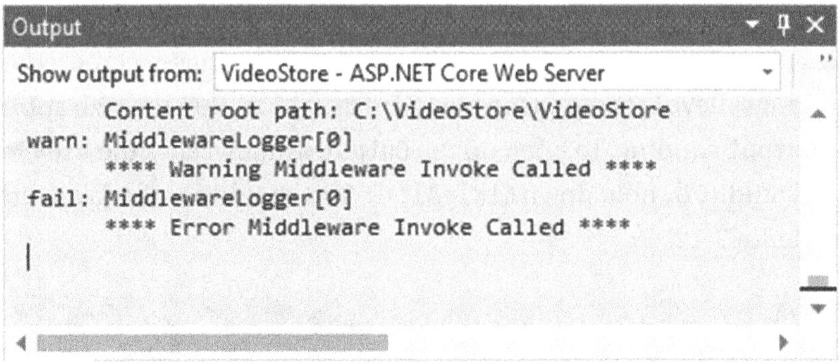

Figure 7-13. *Displaying Only Warnings and Errors*

You might be wondering why we are seeing warning and error logs in the Output window when we just enabled Warning as the default log level. LogLevel specifies the minimum level to create logs for. This means that any logs with a log level greater and equal to warnings will be logged.

The LogLevel indicates the severity of the log. The values range from 0 to 6 and are as follows:

- Trace = 0

- Debug = 1

- Information = 2

- Warning = 3

- Error = 4

- Critical = 5

- None = 6

So at this point, if you are looking at the log level None and wondering why it has a log level of 6, you're not alone. According to the Microsoft Documentation on the LogLevel enum (https://docs.microsoft.com/en-us/dotnet/api/microsoft.extensions.logging.loglevel), None is not used for writing log messages. Scaling up from least critical to most critical, I would probably have started a log level of None at 0, but that's just me.

This means that logging is enabled for the specified level (excluding None) and higher. If you don't specify a LogLevel, then the logging will default to the Information level.

Applying a Specific LogLevel to Production

Taking what we have seen in the previous section, you should be able to understand that we can control what is logged. More specifically, we can control where specific logs are logged from (or rather, from which environments). Looking back at Figure 7-11, you will remember that we have an `appsettings.Production.json` file. Opening up this file, you should see the JSON illustrated in Listing 7-14.

Listing 7-14. The appsettings.Production.json File

```
{
  "Logging": {
    "LogLevel": {
      "Default": "Information",
      "Microsoft": "Warning",
      "Microsoft.Hosting.Lifetime": "Information"
    }
  }
}
```

We are telling ASP.NET Core to log all `Information` log events by default. This is not what I want. In production, I only want to see errors.

It would probably be prudent to log warnings too, but I'm only going to log errors in this example because I want to illustrate the difference between development and production.

Modify the `appsettings.Production.json` file as illustrated in Listing 7-15 by changing the default log level to `Error`.

Listing 7-15. The Modified appsettings.Production.json File

```
{
  "Logging": {
    "LogLevel": {
      "Default": "Error",
```

```
      "Microsoft": "Warning",
      "Microsoft.Hosting.Lifetime": "Information"
    }
  }
}
```

Next, change the default LogLevel in the appsettings.Development.json file back to Information as seen in Listing 7-16.

Listing 7-16. The appsettings.Development.json File

```
{
  "Logging": {
    "LogLevel": {
      "Default": "Information",
      "Microsoft": "Warning",
      "Microsoft.Hosting.Lifetime": "Information"
    }
  }
}
```

Right-click the VideoStore project in your Solution Explorer, and click Properties from the context menu. Then, click the Debug tab.

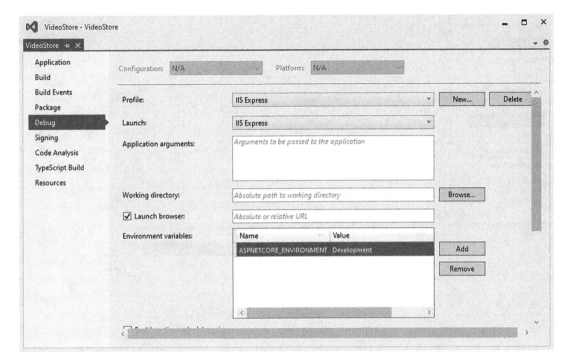

Figure 7-14. *The VideoStore Properties Showing Environment Variables*

You will see (Figure 7-14) that the current ASPNETCORE_ENVIRONMENT variable is set to Development.

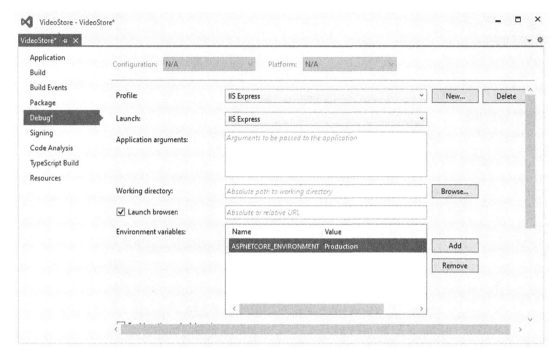

Figure 7-15. *The Modified Environment Variable*

Change the ASPNETCORE_ENVIRONMENT variable to Production, and save the settings (Figure 7-15). With this setting changed, the web application will run as it would in a production environment. Go ahead and debug your application.

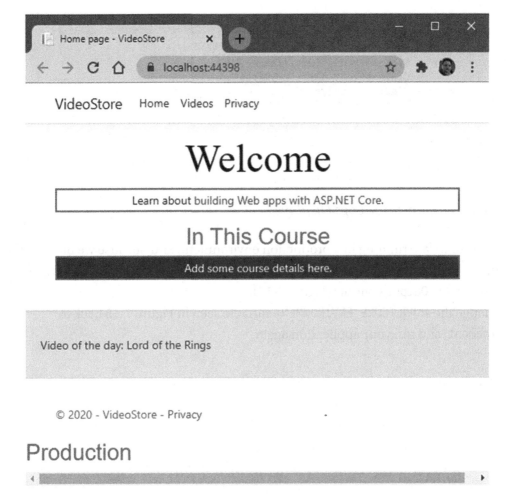

Figure 7-16. *The Web Application Running in the Production Environment*

As seen in Figure 7-16, the web application now runs as if it is in a production environment.

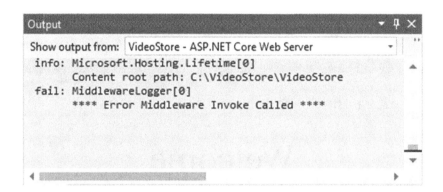

Figure 7-17. *Only Error Logs Displayed*

Because we are running in a production environment, and because we have set the default log level in the `appsettings.Production.json` file to `Error`, we will only see error logs in the `Output` window (Figure 7-17).

Change the `ASPNETCORE_ENVIRONMENT` variable seen in Figure 7-15 back to `Development`, and run your application again.

Figure 7-18. *The Web Application Running in the Development Environment*

As seen in Figure 7-18, the web application now runs as if it is in a development environment.

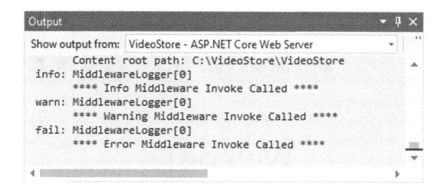

Figure 7-19. *Information, Warnings, and Error Messages Displayed*

Because we are running in a development environment, and because we have set the default log level in the `appsettings.Development.json` file to `Information`, we will see information logs and higher in the `Output` window (Figure 7-19).

A Quick Look at the Log Category

When you have a look at the `VideoError.cshtml.cs` class, you will see that we added the `ILogger` to the class via dependency injection. When we force an error on the Video Detail page, you will see that the category name of the log message (which is `VideoStore.Pages.Videos.VideoErrorModel`) in the Output window is the fully qualified type name.

This is because ASP.NET Core uses `ILogger<T>` to get an instance of `ILogger` that uses the fully qualified type name of T. Seeing as we use `ILogger<VideoErrorModel>`, we get the fully qualified type name as the log category in the `Output` window.

This is in contrast to the logger we created in the `MyCustomMiddleware` class. There we used an `ILoggerFactory` and specified the category name as `MiddlewareLogger`. This is then is the category name we see in the `Output` window. Just refer back to Figure 7-9 where you can see the two different log categories displayed in the `Output` window.

Therefore, if you need to specify the name of your log category, then an `ILoggerFactory` is the way to go. The string you specify for the category name is arbitrary, but by convention, you should use the class name.

Wrapping Up

Logging in .NET Core and ASP.NET Core is quite a large topic to cover in only a single chapter. You can use third-party logging providers if the built-in logging providers don't meet your needs. You can also go ahead and create your own custom logger if you need to. Another interesting thing to note is that you can specify event IDs for your logs. I encourage you to spend some time reading up more on logging in .NET Core.

For a complete document on logging in ASP.NET Core, view the documentation on Microsoft Docs: `https://docs.microsoft.com/en-us/aspnet/core/fundamentals/logging/?view=aspnetcore-3.1`.

CHAPTER 8

Web Application Deployment

The final step in any web application is to publish and deploy it to some sort of server. Depending on the workflow you (or your company) follows, this job might not even be something you as a developer would typically do. Based on pull requests and releases, you might end up with a version of the web application that is ready for deployment. That deployment might, however, be the job of someone in your team that is responsible for putting the published files on a server for UAT. Once UAT has passed, it can be put into production.

Please note, this chapter assumes that you have a copy of SQL Server Management Studio already installed. If not, refer to the following document: `https://docs.microsoft.com/en-us/sql/ssms/download-sql-server-management-studio-ssms`.

You might be the only web developer in your organization and solely responsible for the development and deployment of your web application. Whatever your current workflow is, in this chapter, we will take a look at deploying your web application to a local IIS server and connecting to a local SQL Server instance.

Getting Your Site Ready for Deployment

Before we publish the web application, I want to temporarily remove the logic in the `ConfigureServices` method that uses the `SQLData` class in the `VideoStore.Data` project. I want to focus on getting the published files working with IIS and worry about configuring the database after I know that the site is running.

© Dirk Strauss 2021
D. Strauss, *Creating ASP.NET Core Web Applications*, https://doi.org/10.1007/978-1-4842-6828-5_8

Listing 8-1. The Temporarily Modified Configure Services Method

```
public void ConfigureServices(IServiceCollection services)
{
    _ = services.AddDbContextPool<VideoDbContext>(dbContextOptns =>
    {
        _ = dbContextOptns.UseSqlServer(
            Configuration.GetConnectionString("VideoConn"));
    });

    //_ = services.AddScoped<IVideoData, SQLData>();
    _ = services.AddSingleton<IVideoData, TestData>(); // TODO: Change to
                                                       scoped
    _ = services.AddRazorPages().AddSessionStateTempDataProvider();
    _ = services.AddSession();
}
```

As seen in Listing 8-1, I have commented out the code that uses the SQLData class when an instance of IVideoData is required and replaced it with the TestData class. Now let's work on publishing the web application.

To be able to deploy your web application, you will first need to publish your files. This step takes your web application and puts all the required files in a location you choose. From there, you can deploy those files to a web server environment. This is when we publish to a local folder.

As seen in Figure 8-1, there are other options available for you as a developer when right-clicking your VideoStore project and selecting Publish from the context menu.

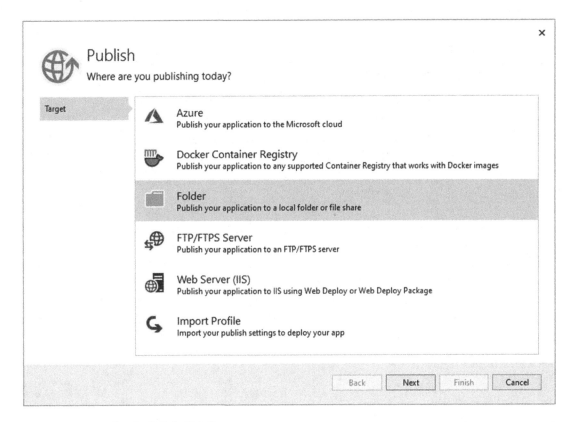

Figure 8-1. *The Publish Dialog*

We will just be publishing our web application to a local folder, but you can perform a publish and deploy by selecting Azure, IIS, and so on. Clicking Next, you are allowed to specify a path to publish to. I have selected C:\temp\videostore_publish as seen in Figure 8-2.

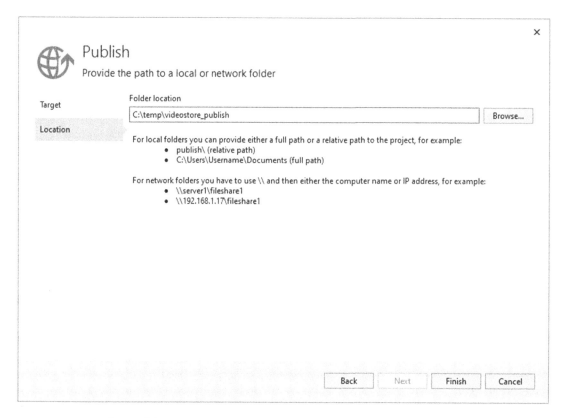

Figure 8-2. *The Publish Output Location*

With the publish path set, click the Finish button.

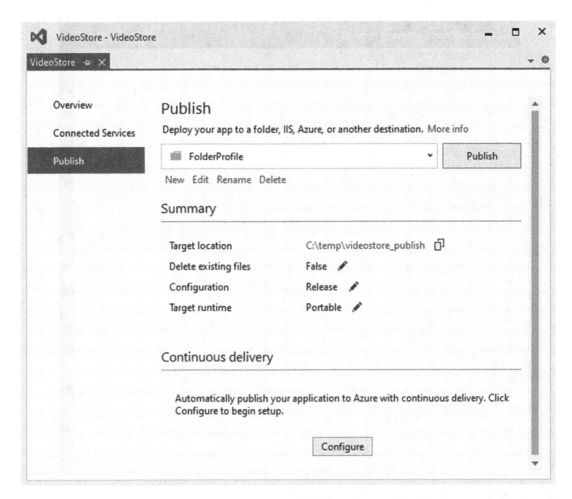

Figure 8-3. *The Publish Screen*

You are now presented with the Publish screen (Figure 8-3) in Visual Studio. You can modify some of the settings here such as renaming the publish profile you just set up, changing the configuration, target runtime, and opting to delete existing files in the publish folder.

We aren't going to do any of that. We simply want to publish our web application. To do that, just click the Publish button, and Visual Studio will start to build the required files and copy them to the output folder you selected.

After the publish has been completed, you will see the compiled files (the DLLs) in your publish folder along with all the dependencies and configuration files.

You can also publish the web application from the command line. From the Command Prompt, navigate to the folder where your .csproj file is.

```
Administrator: Command Prompt                              —      □      ✕
C:\videostore\VideoStore>dir
 Volume in drive C is OS_Install
 Volume Serial Number is 4A81-4980

 Directory of C:\videostore\VideoStore

2020/12/24  08:28    <DIR>          .
2020/12/24  08:28    <DIR>          ..
2020/12/20  11:00              159 appsettings.Development.json
2020/11/12  08:52              387 appsettings.json
2020/12/20  11:34              168 appsettings.Production.json
2020/12/24  08:28    <DIR>          bin
2020/12/12  12:34              107 compilerconfig.json
2020/12/12  12:28            1 321 compilerconfig.json.defaults
2020/12/19  16:28    <DIR>          CustomMiddleware
2020/12/24  08:28    <DIR>          obj
2020/12/24  08:28    <DIR>          Pages
2020/12/21  08:54              889 Program.cs
2020/12/24  08:28    <DIR>          Properties
2020/12/19  16:19            3 031 Startup.cs
2020/12/19  12:54    <DIR>          StaticFiles
2020/11/22  11:08    <DIR>          TagHelpers
2020/12/19  15:55              975 VideoStore.csproj
2020/12/23  09:00            1 075 VideoStore.csproj.user
2020/11/28  17:27    <DIR>          ViewComponents
2020/12/24  08:28    <DIR>          wwwroot
               9 File(s)          8 112 bytes
              11 Dir(s)   121 644 879 872 bytes free

C:\videostore\VideoStore>
```

Figure 8-4. *The Location of the csproj File*

Running the dir command will display the contents of your current folder (Figure 8-4). Here, you will see the Startup.cs, the Program.cs, and the csproj file for our project. Now, run the command in Listing 8-2.

Listing 8-2. The dotnet publish Command

```
dotnet publish -o c:\temp\videostore_publish
```

You will notice that we specify the output directory by using -o in the publish command. The publish will start and copy the compiled files to the output directory specified (Figure 8-5).

```
C:\videostore\VideoStore>dotnet publish -o c:\temp\videostore_publish
Microsoft (R) Build Engine version 16.6.0+5ff7b0c9e for .NET Core
Copyright (C) Microsoft Corporation. All rights reserved.

  Determining projects to restore...
  Restored C:\videostore\VideoStore.Core\VideoStore.Core.csproj (in 177 ms).
  Restored C:\videostore\VideoStore.Data\VideoStore.Data.csproj (in 442 ms).
  Restored C:\videostore\VideoStore\VideoStore.csproj (in 471 ms).
  VideoStore.Core -> C:\videostore\VideoStore.Core\bin\Debug\netcoreapp3.1\VideoStore.Core.dll
  VideoStore.Data -> C:\videostore\VideoStore.Data\bin\Debug\netcoreapp3.1\VideoStore.Data.dll
  VideoStore -> C:\videostore\VideoStore\bin\Debug\netcoreapp3.1\VideoStore.dll
  VideoStore -> C:\videostore\VideoStore\bin\Debug\netcoreapp3.1\VideoStore.Views.dll
  VideoStore -> c:\temp\videostore_publish\

C:\videostore\VideoStore>
```

Figure 8-5. Publish the Web Application from the Command Line

From the Command Prompt, you can type `dotnet publish --help` to see the options available when using publish from the command line. The usage is defined as `dotnet publish [options] <PROJECT | SOLUTION>`. The `<PROJECT | SOLUTION>` arguments specify which project or solution file to operate on. In our example, we didn't have to specify a directory, seeing as we were in the directory where the `csproj` file was located. This means that the `dotnet publish` command will search the current directory.

The options available to use with the publish command are

- `-h, --help` – Show command line help.

- `-o, --output <OUTPUT_DIR>` – The output directory to place the published artifacts in.

- `-f, --framework <FRAMEWORK>` – The target framework to publish for. The target framework has to be specified in the project file.

- `-r, --runtime <RUNTIME_IDENTIFIER>` – The target runtime to publish for. This is used when creating a self-contained deployment. The default is to publish a framework-dependent application.

- `-c, --configuration <CONFIGURATION>` – The configuration to publish for. The default for most projects is "Debug."

- `--version-suffix <VERSION_SUFFIX>` – Set the value of the $(VersionSuffix) property to use when building the project.

263

- `--manifest <MANIFEST>` – The path to a target manifest file that contains the list of packages to be excluded from the publish step.

- `--no-build` – Do not build the project before publishing. Implies `--no-restore`.

- `--self-contained` – Publish the .NET Core runtime with your application so the runtime doesn't need to be installed on the target machine. The default is "true" if a runtime identifier is specified.

- `--no-self-contained` – Publish your application as a framework-dependent application without the .NET Core runtime. A supported .NET Core runtime must be installed to run your application.

- `/nologo, --nologo` – Do not display the startup banner or the copyright message.

- `--interactive` – Allows the command to stop and wait for user input or action (e.g., to complete authentication).

- `--no-restore` – Do not restore the project before building.

- `-v, --verbosity <LEVEL>` – Set the MSBuild verbosity level. Allowed values are q[uiet], m[inimal], n[ormal], d[etailed], and diag[nostic].

- `--no-dependencies` – Do not restore project-to-project references and only restore the specified project.

- `--force` – Force all dependencies to be resolved even if the last restore was successful. This is equivalent to deleting project.assets. json.

Once the process has been completed, the compiled files will be copied to the output directory as specified with the `-o` option. For a good reference on the `dotnet publish` command, see this article on Microsoft Docs: `https://docs.microsoft.com/en-us/dotnet/core/tools/dotnet-publish`.

Deploying Your Web Application to IIS

To start the deployment process, open up Internet Information Services (IIS) Manager.

You can also click Start, and enter `inetmgr` in the Search box, and press Enter.

With the manager open, click the server. As seen in Figure 8-6, mine is called `MSI` (`MSI\Dirk Strauss`). Make sure that you have the `Features View` selected at the bottom of the screen.

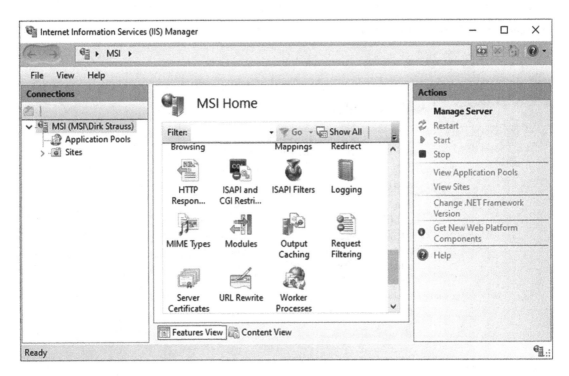

Figure 8-6. *IIS Manager*

Search for the `Modules` section which is contained under the IIS grouping. You can see the `Modules` section in Figure 8-6, the second row, second from the left. Click the `Modules` section to display a list of installed modules.

Modules are added to a server so that you can provide some additional desired functionality to applications. Modules can be added, edited, configured, or removed from the Modules section.

The specific module that we are looking for is the AspNetCoreModuleV2 which is the .NET Core Hosting Bundle (Figure 8-7). It allows ASP.NET Core apps to run with IIS, and if you do not see it listed in the Modules section of IIS, you will need to install it before you can deploy your application to IIS.

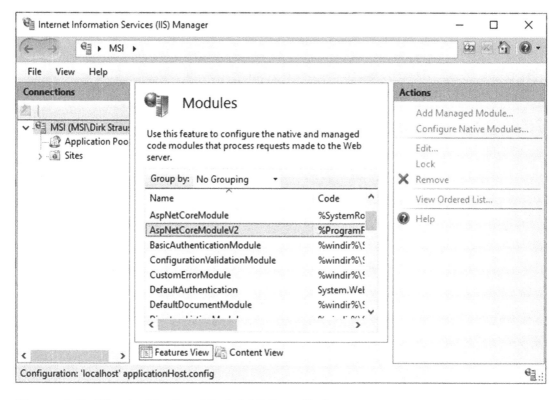

Figure 8-7.   *The AspNetCoreModuleV2 Installed*

To find the download for the .NET Core Hosting Bundle, find the Microsoft Docs page for The .NET Core Hosting Bundle, and find the direct download link on the page. At the time of writing this book, the download link was as follows: https://dotnet. microsoft.com/download/dotnet-core/thank-you/runtime-aspnetcore-5.0.1-windows-hosting-bundle-installer.

Please note that a restart of IIS might be required after installing the hosting bundle.

Once the .NET Core Hosting Bundle is installed, right-click the Sites folder, and click Add Website as seen in Figure 8-8.

Figure 8-8. *Add a Website*

You might see the default website listed here, but we are adding a new site called VideoStore to the server.

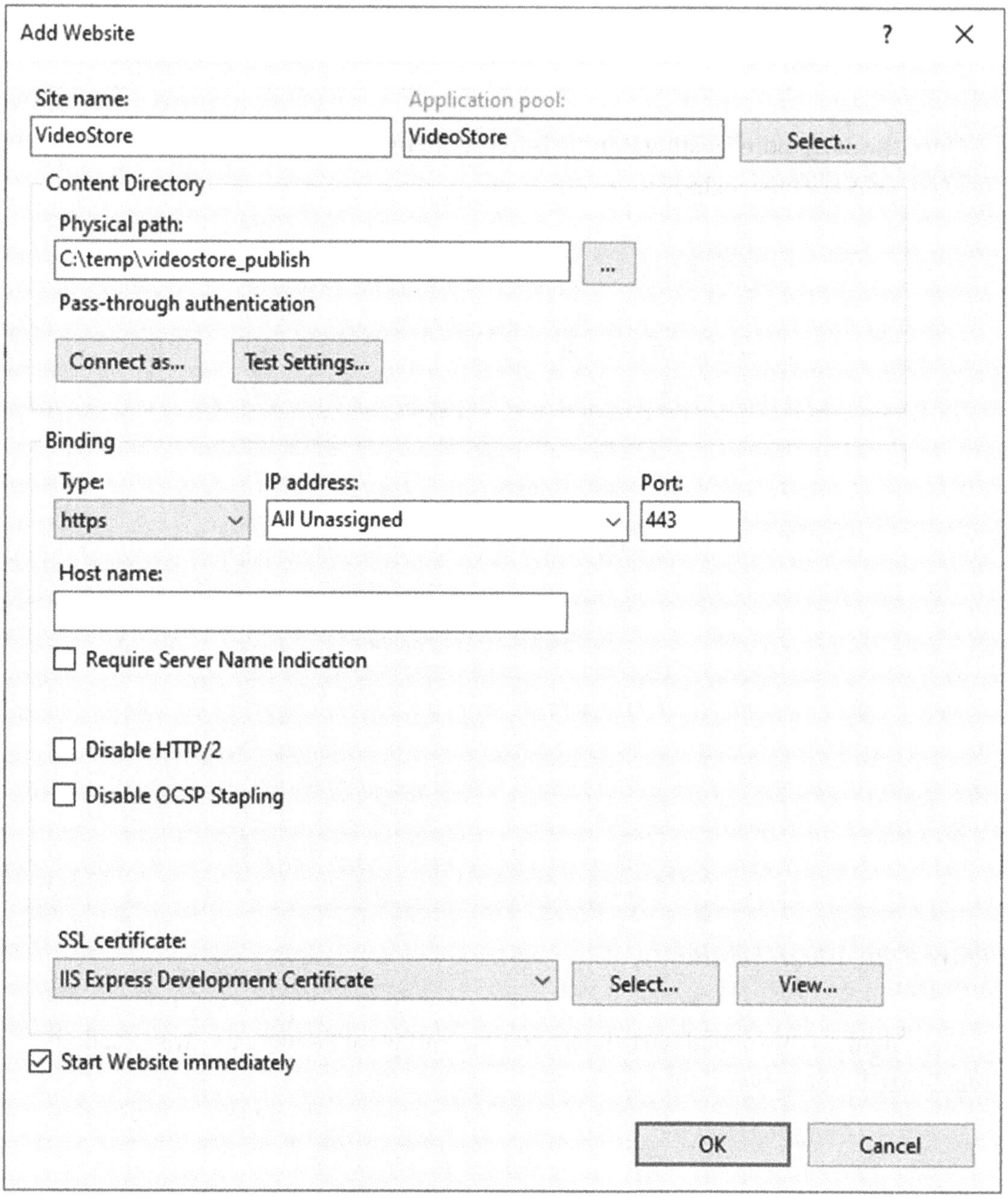

Figure 8-9. *The Add Website Window*

From the Add Website window (Figure 8-9), you will need to give your website a site name. I have just called the site VideoStore. The physical path is simply the location of the folder that we published the web application to. Generally, I don't like doing this and prefer to put the published files in a specific folder other than the temp folder. Because I'm only on my local IIS, I'm going to be a bit sneaky here and leave it pointing to the publishing folder.

The benefit of placing the published files into a specific folder on the server is that you can lock the folder down as required for your organization with the relevant permissions and constraints.

The other setting we are changing on this window is the binding type. By default, it is HTTP, but we want HTTPS. Change the binding type, and leave the default port at 443. Being on our local IIS, and because this is a development machine, I am going to select the IIS Express Development Certificate under the SSL certificate drop-down. When you deploy to a live server, you would want to install a proper SSL certificate for your website and would never select a development certificate as we have done here.

Lastly, we want to select the option to start the website immediately and then click the OK button.

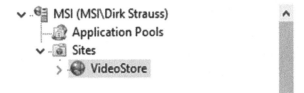

Figure 8-10. *The Added VideoStore Site*

The VideoStore web application is now created in IIS and ready (Figure 8-10). Open up your browser and type in the URL for the site which is https://localhost.

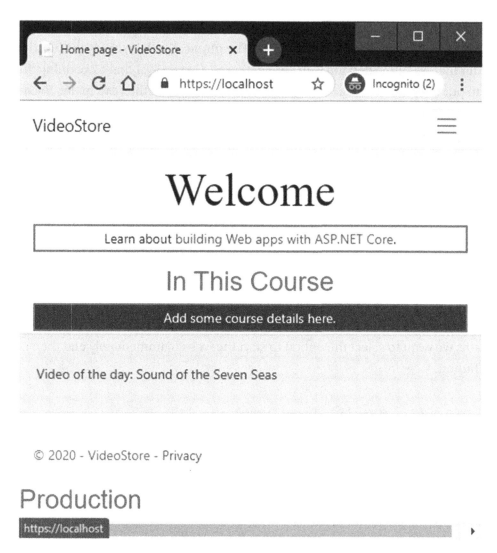

Figure 8-11. *The Deployed VideoStore Site*

As seen in Figure 8-11, the deployed VideoStore site is now available and running on localhost using HTTPS. You will also notice that the word Production is displayed in the footer of the site because the web application is now deployed.

Configuring the SQL Server Database

To set up our web application to connect to a SQL Server database, we can use one of many methods. This chapter is not going to serve as an exhaustive list of methods to configure the site to connect to SQL Server. The method you use will depend on your specific situation. In this book, however, we will simply create the database and configure the application to connect to it.

Start by changing the ConfigureServices method back to use the SQLData class as seen in Listing 8-3.

Listing 8-3. Adding in the SQLData Class Back

```
public void ConfigureServices(IServiceCollection services)
{
    _ = services.AddDbContextPool<VideoDbContext>(dbContextOptns =>
    {
        _ = dbContextOptns.UseSqlServer(
            Configuration.GetConnectionString("VideoConn"));
    });

    _ = services.AddScoped<IVideoData, SQLData>();
    //_ = services.AddSingleton<IVideoData, TestData>(); // TODO: Change to
                                                         scoped
    _ = services.AddRazorPages().AddSessionStateTempDataProvider();
    _ = services.AddSession();
}
```

If you had to stop the VideoStore web app in IIS, publish the site, and start the VideoStore web app in IIS, the site will not work (Figure 8-12) when you go to https://localhost.

The reason for this is that we are telling the application to use a SQL database, and in the appsettings.Production.json file, we have nothing listed for the connection string.

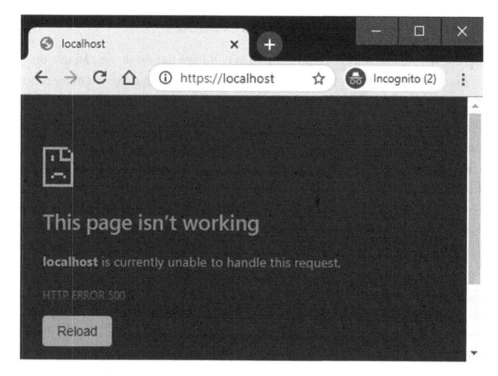

Figure 8-12. *Error 500 on Localhost*

Let's start resolving these issues one at a time. The first thing we need is a database. We can generate this database create script by running the `dotnet ef migrations script` command in Listing 8-4. Ensure that you are in the `VideoStore.Data` project in the Command Prompt.

Listing 8-4. Run the ef migrations script Command

```
dotnet ef migrations script -s ..\VideoStore\VideoStore.csproj -o c:\temp\
scripts\VideoStoreCreateScript.sql
```

As we have seen earlier in this book, the command specifies the startup project by telling `dotnet` where the `csproj` file is located using the `-s` option.

We also specify an output directory for the create script by supplying a path after the `-o` option.

After running the command, you will see the output as illustrated in Figure 8-13. Navigating to the output folder you specified, you will see the created `VideoStoreCreateScript.sql` file.

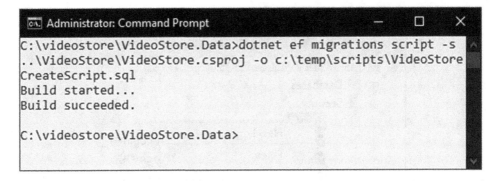

Figure 8-13. *The ef migrations script Command Run*

Next, open up SQL Server Management Studio, and create a new database called VideoStoreLive. Run the VideoStoreCreateScript.sql file against the newly created database to create tables.

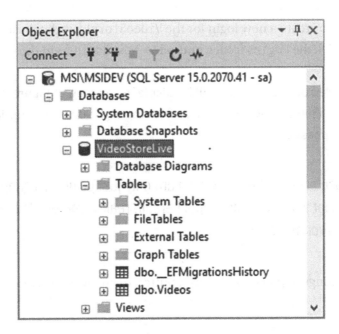

Figure 8-14. *The Created SQL Database*

Refreshing the database and expanding the tables folder, you will see the created tables (Figure 8-14).

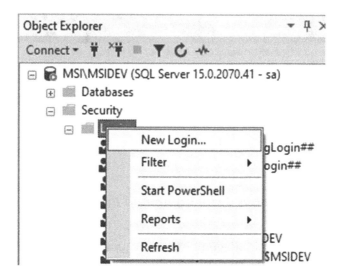

Figure 8-15. *Create a New Login*

We now need to create a new login for the VideoStoreLive database. Under Security, right-click the Logins folder, and select New Login from the context menu (Figure 8-15).

The Login - New dialog window will be displayed as seen in Figure 8-16. For the login name, give it a name of videostore and (using SQL Server authentication) a password of videopassword.

Please do not use such bad passwords. I am only just using this simple password because we're just illustrating concepts here. In reality, you wouldn't ever do this in a production environment.

With these settings in place, click the OK button to create the login.

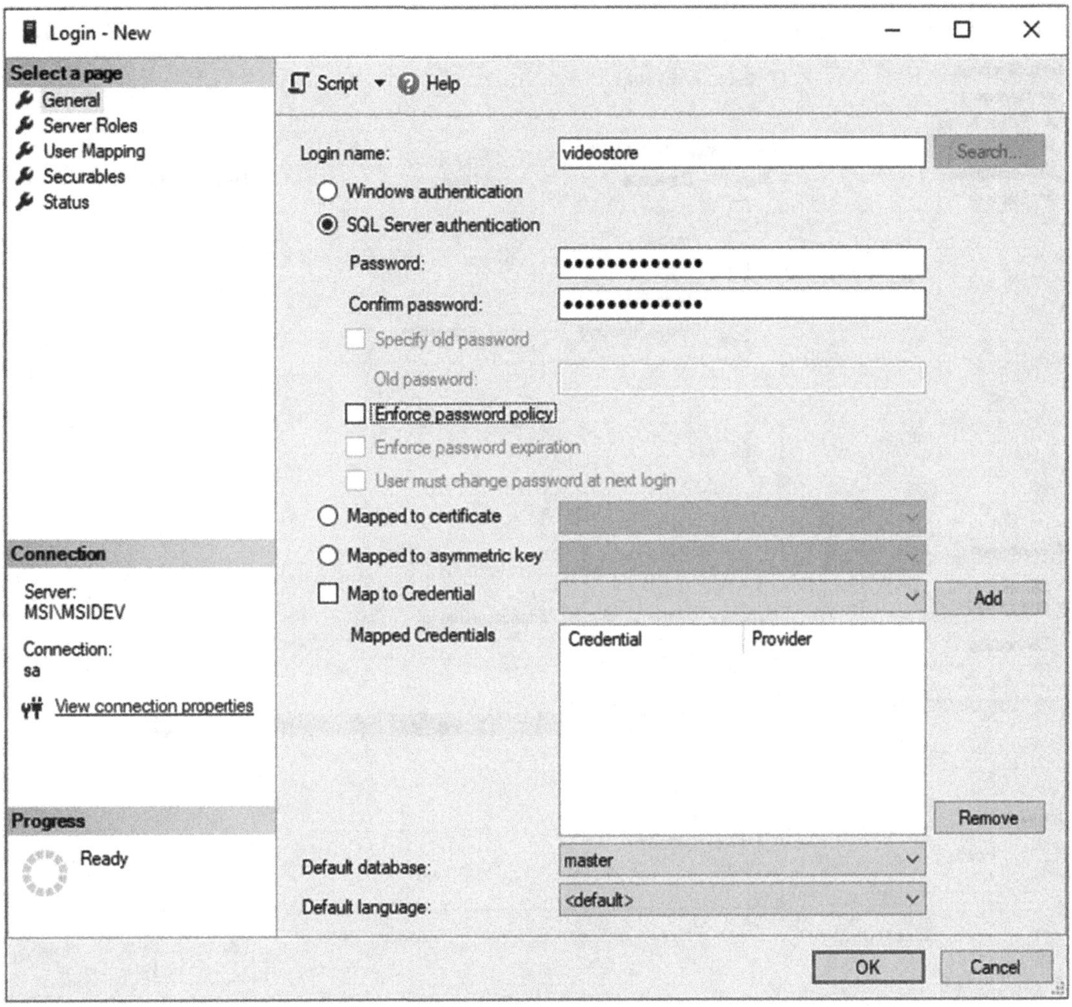

Figure 8-16. *Create Login Name and Password*

You will see the newly created login in the list. Right-click the created `videostore` login, and select `Properties` from the context menu.

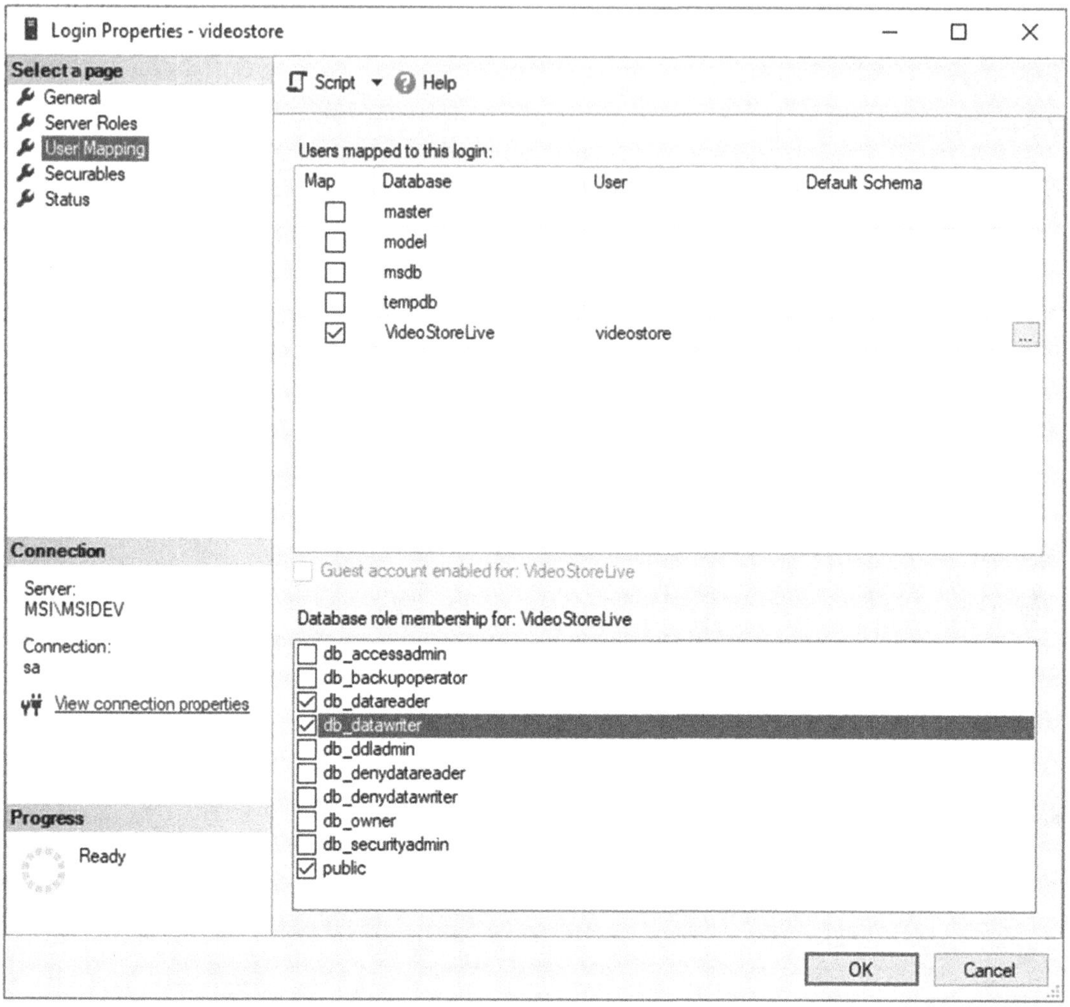

Figure 8-17. *Modify Login User Mappings*

Modify the User Mapping (Figure 8-17) for the videostore login by selecting the VideoStoreLive database as the map and the role memberships as db_datareader and db_datawriter. The next thing we want to do is modify the appsettings. Production.json, appsettings.Development.json, and appsettings.json files as illustrated in Listings 8-5, 8-6, and 8-7, respectively.

We are moving the connection string that points to localdb used in development to the appsettings.Development.json file and creating a live connection string to the VideoStoreLive database in the appsettings.Production.json file.

Listing 8-5. The Production appsettings File

```
{
  "Logging": {
    "LogLevel": {
      "Default": "Information",
      "Microsoft": "Warning",
      "Microsoft.Hosting.Lifetime": "Information"
    }
  },
  "ConnectionStrings": {
    "VideoConn": "Data Source=MSI\\MSIDEV;Initial Catalog=VideoStoreLive;
    Integrated Security=False;User Id=videostore;Password=videopassword"
  }
}
```

Listing 8-6. The Development appsettings File

```
{
  "Logging": {
    "LogLevel": {
      "Default": "Information",
      "Microsoft": "Warning",
      "Microsoft.Hosting.Lifetime": "Information"
    }
  },
  "ConnectionStrings": {
    "VideoConn": "Data Source=(localdb)\\MSSQLLocalDB;Initial
    Catalog=VideoStore;Integrated Security=True;"
  }
}
```

Listing 8-7. The appsettings.json File

```
{
  "Logging": {
    "LogLevel": {
      "Default": "Information",
      "Microsoft": "Warning",
      "Microsoft.Hosting.Lifetime": "Information"
    }
  },
  "AllowedHosts": "*",
  "VideoListPageTitle": "Video Store - Videos List"
}
```

If you're wondering about storing credentials in the `appsettings` file, your hesitation here is correct. I'll discuss this at the end of the chapter.

You will notice that the `appsettings.json` file no longer contains a connection string. Depending on if we are running in development, or production, our application will use the correct `appsettings` file.

Now we can publish the site again. Stop the `VideoStore` web app in IIS by clicking the `Stop` button in the `Manage Website` panel. Publish site again by running the `dotnet publish` command as seen in Listing 8-2. In the output folder for the published files, check that the production appsettings file is present. If it is (it should be), start the `VideoStore` web app in IIS.

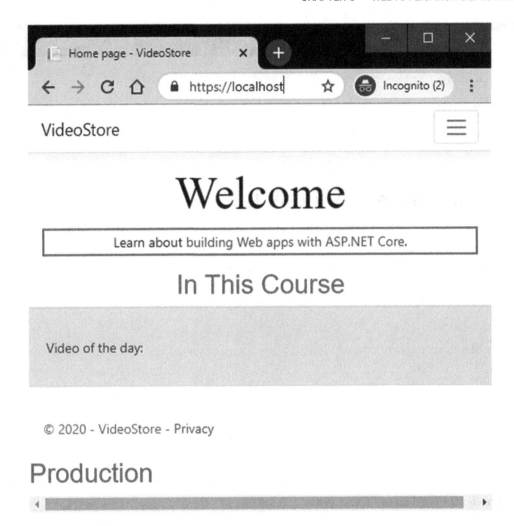

Figure 8-18. *VideoStore Site Running Against VideoStoreLive Database*

Now, run your web application again in the browser. You should see Figure 8-18. If you look at the Video of the day, you will see an empty notification.

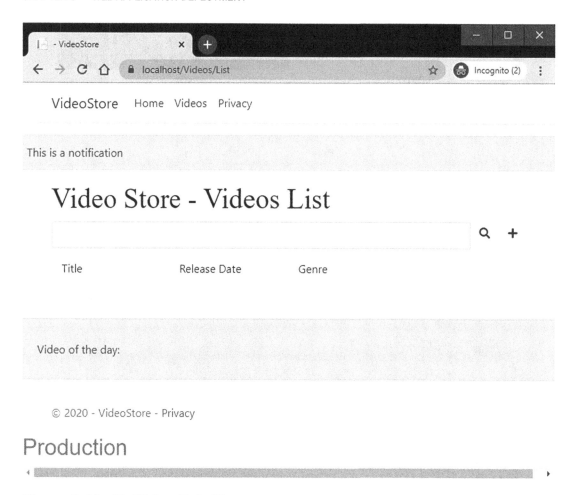

Figure 8-19. *No Videos Exist Yet*

The reason for this is that we are now running against the SQL Server database, and that database contains no videos. When we navigate to the list of videos, we will see no videos listed (Figure 8-19).

Let's create our first video by clicking the + button next to the video search.

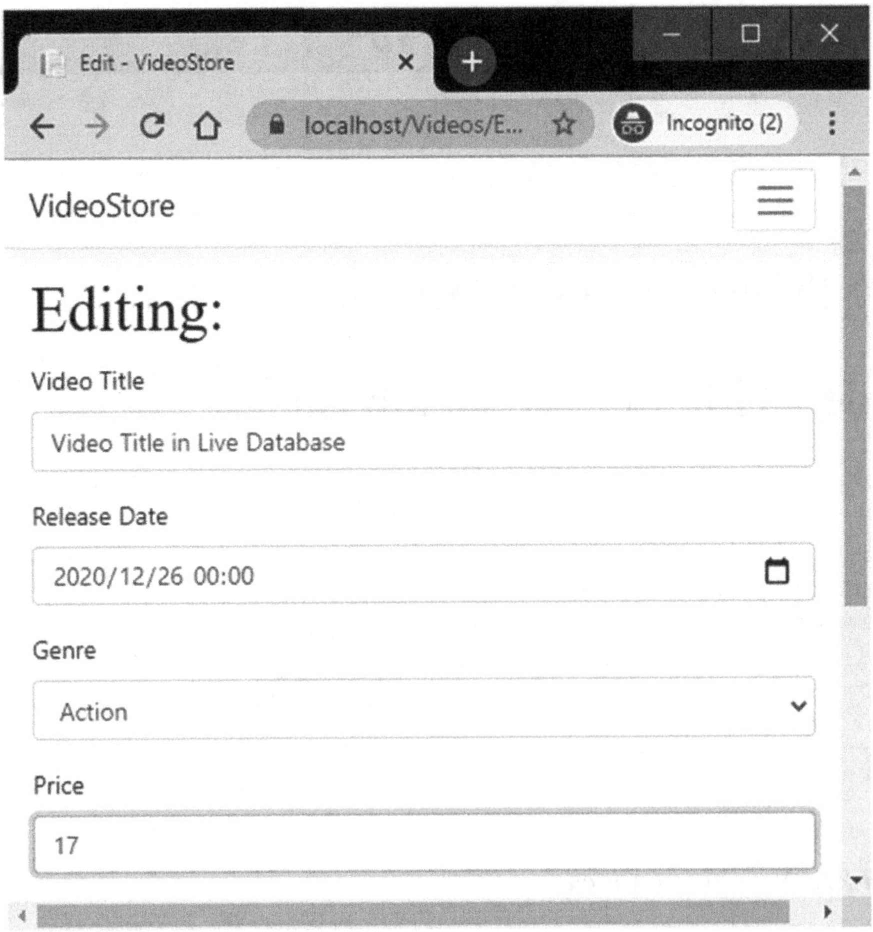

Figure 8-20. *Adding a New Video*

We can now add a new video to our Video Store as seen in Figure 8-20.

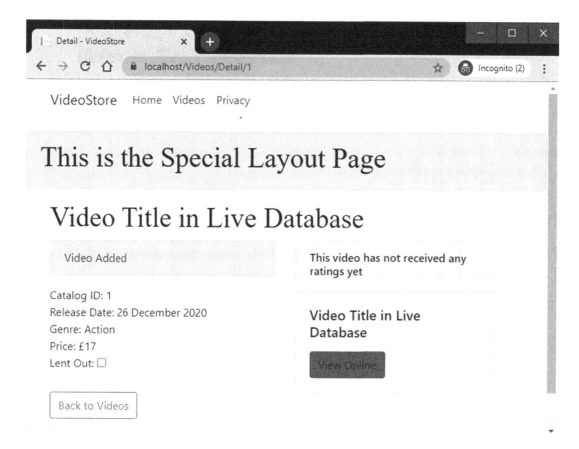

Figure 8-21. *New Video Added*

When the new video is added, we are taken to the Video Detail page as seen in Figure 8-21.

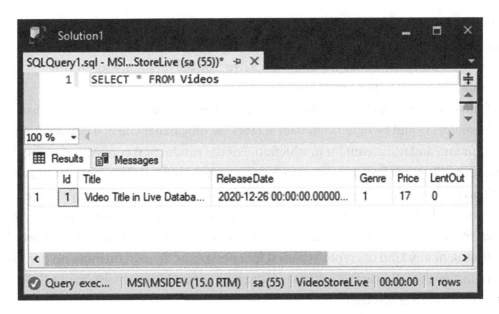

Figure 8-22. *Viewing the Newly Added Video in MS SQL Server*

Swing over to SQL Server Management Studio, and run SELECT * FROM Videos
against the VideoStoreLive database. You will see the newly added video in the SQL
database (Figure 8-22).

This is all that is needed to deploy a web application to a server running IIS. It is
quite straightforward, and there are other methods you can use to get your database
created using dotnet migrations. The approach illustrated in this chapter is but one way
of deploying the web application.

Lastly, a short note on managing user secrets and connection strings.

A Note About Connection Strings and Secrets

Earlier in this chapter, in Code Listings 8-5, 8-6, and 8-7, we used the development and
production appsettings to store the different connection strings. The problem with this
approach is that these files invariably end up in your source code repository. That isn't a
good thing.

The reason I added the live database connection string to the appsettings.
Production.json file is to illustrate the fact that the application is using different
settings based on the environment it finds itself in. In reality, you would not be adding
connection strings containing user credentials to your config files at all.

Because we are using integrated security for the localdb connection in the `appsettings.Development.json` file, storing the connection in this manner didn't matter. Now, however, we are working with a live SQL Server database. Storing credentials like this is not acceptable.

If you had user credentials in the connection string to the localdb, then the use of user secrets would be beneficial. User secrets are only beneficial in a development environment, and not meant for production. For the production connection string, keeping the file clean from any user credentials is the way to go. The connection can be configured in the appsettings file on the server itself. There are various ways to keep user credentials safe. One of these is by using the Azure Key Vault. Azure Key Vault is a cloud service for safely and securely storing any kind of secret, be that an API key, passwords, certificates, or any kind of crypto key used for encryption. To read up more on the Azure Key Vault, see the following link: `https://docs.microsoft.com/en-us/azure/key-vault/general/basic-concepts`.

For more information on securely storing application secrets while in development, refer to the following Microsoft Document on user secrets: `https://docs.microsoft.com/en-us/aspnet/core/security/app-secrets`.

Index

A

AddVideo Method, 110

appsettings.Development.json file, 241, 242, 245, 248, 284

appsettings.json file, 240, 278
- configuration file, 20, 21
- modified listmodel class, 22

appsettings.Production.json file, 247, 283

asp-for tag helper, 50, 52, 89

ASPNETCORE_ENVIRONMENT variable, 187, 250

asp-page tag helper, 59

asp-route tag helper, 62

asp-validation-for tag helper, 99, 104

B

Bad requests handling
- DetailModel, 76
- error page, 73
- generic error page, 74
- incorrect Video ID, 77
- OnGet method, 77
- VideoError markup, 75
- VideoErrorModel class, 76
- VideoError page, 75, 78

Base padding value, 209

BindProperty attribute, 50, 76

Button tag helpers, 61

C

Chrome developer tools
- adding and modifying styles, 215–218
- dragging elements, 213, 215
- new class adding, 218, 219
- page markup, 213
- testing state changes, 219, 220
- throttling network speed, 221–223

CommitMessage, 112, 114

Compiled CSS, 204

compilerconfig.json file, 195

Configure method, 225

ConfigureServices
- method, 33, 34, 101, 116, 130, 133, 257, 271

Connection strings, 129, 283

CreateDefaultBuilder method, 243

custom.css file, 198

Custom Middleware
- class added, 234
- class boilerplate code, 234
- log messages, 238
- modified configure method, 237
- modified custom middleware class, 235
- modified InvokeAsync method, 244
- template, 233

Custom SCSS file added, 191

Custom TagHelper, 161–165

D

W, X, Y, Z

Printed in the United States
By Bookmasters